I Am
Charlotte

Charlotte Gober Czekala

Order this book online at www.trafford.com
or email orders@trafford.com

Most Trafford titles are also available at major online book retailers.

My thanks to Thomas Nelson for allowing me to use the quotation from Jesus Calling.

Printed in the United States of America.

ISBN: 978-1-4669-6338-2 (sc)
ISBN: 978-1-4669-6337-5 (hc)
ISBN: 978-1-4669-6336-8 (e)

Library of Congress Control Number: 2012921119

Trafford rev. 09/03/2014

 www.trafford.com

North America & international
toll-free: 1 888 232 4444 (USA & Canada)
fax: 812 355 4082

Contents

PREFACE

This is the story of my life told as best as I can remember. I guess the main reason that I wanted to write an autobiography was my interest in history and the desire to know more about the people that were a part of it. I suppose we value those things that we cannot replace, and I was not able to gain insight into the lives of my ancestors. Oh, how I wish I had asked my grandmothers more and written it down. I started getting really interested in my genealogy about the time I was homeschooling my two eldest granddaughters, Kelley and Jessica. We would go out to the archives in East Point, Georgia, and I would look up all the different relatives on reels of microfiche. Yes, this was before the information was so readily available on the Internet. Just seeing some of the papers that my ancestors had signed was so interesting to me. I wanted to know more. Therefore, I didn't want any of my posterity to be in the same boat as I. So here it is—maybe a little long at times—but I also wanted to *weave* in a little of the history that was being made as I was living my life—my desire to let you have a picture into the walk of faith I have had with my Heavenly Father.

Please enjoy your visit with me in this account of my life.

ACKNOWLEDGMENTS

W here do I start with thanking the people who have helped me write this book? By the way, I started with a paper at Kennesaw State University and ended with a book. Well, my excuse for its being so long is the fact that a lot happens during seven decades. First to thank are the many teachers who taught me just to write. Then there are those specific people; and immediately, I think of my cousin Dodger, who has an amazing memory of our early life on the farm. Dodger, along with my nephew, Chuck; husband, Bob; son, Lane; and even my tennis partner, Jackie Huff, helped me remember what happened during certain periods in my life. Also, my cousin Beckie and daughter-in law Karon, who gave many hours editing and giving me suggestions to improve my book.

The reader may not realize how I have benefited from having Word on my computer instead of having to type and then make changes with an eraser! Technology is wonderful and has advanced so much since my early school days. Of course, I used Google and many other sites where I obtained the real facts on my wonderful pink Sony VAIO computer. Then followed the Asus computer after I burned up the VAIO! I am still not the great computer expert.

Thank the Lord for giving me the desire to keep everything that was ever important to me in boxes and filing cabinets stashed away all over the house. Even if it drove Bob nuts, there was a reason that I just couldn't throw anything away! Many dates were there just waiting to be found in all those calendars that I had kept for thirty years.

Also, the many autobiographies that I have loved reading over the years certainly gave me some insight and desire to do the same. I am grateful.

This book is dedicated to:

The Triune God: Father, Son, and Holy Spirit; also, to my husband, Bob, who has faithfully shared my life for over 50 years; and our two sons, Ken and Lane, who brought us much joy and then challenges, which God used to draw me closer and more dependent on Him.

In memory of my mother and daddy who loved me so much.

Maternal Family Tree

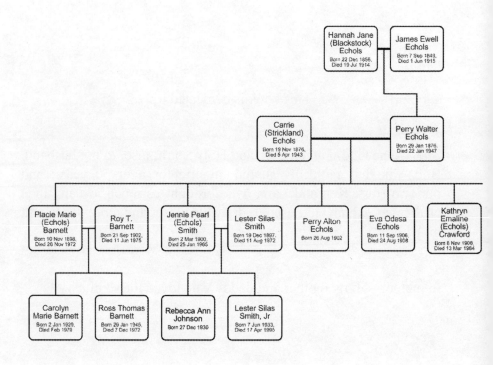

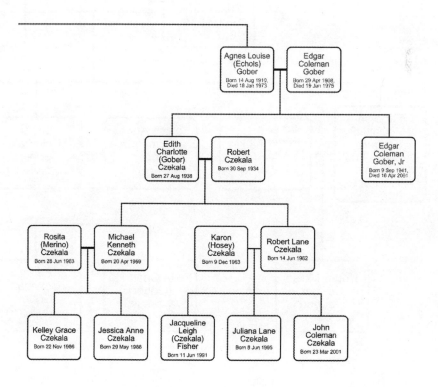

Paternal Family Tree

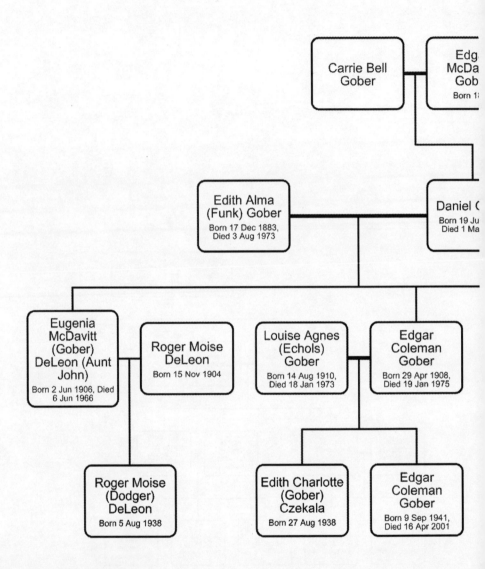

Carrie Bell Gober

Edg
McDa
Gob
Born 1:

Edith Alma (Funk) Gober
Born 17 Dec 1883, Died 3 Aug 1973

Daniel (
Born 19 Ju
Died 1 Ma

Eugenia McDavitt (Gober) DeLeon (Aunt John)
Born 2 Jun 1906, Died 6 Jun 1966

Roger Moise DeLeon
Born 15 Nov 1904

Louise Agnes (Echols) Gober
Born 14 Aug 1910, Died 18 Jan 1973

Edgar Coleman Gober
Born 29 Apr 1908, Died 19 Jan 1975

Roger Moise (Dodger) DeLeon
Born 5 Aug 1938

Edith Charlotte (Gober) Czekala
Born 27 Aug 1938

Edgar Coleman Gober
Born 9 Sep 1941, Died 16 Apr 2001

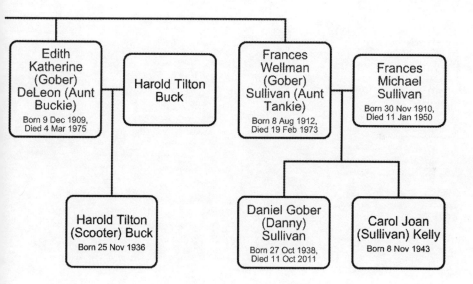

ar
vviltt
er
855

Gober
n 1883,
y 1951

Edith Katherine (Gober) DeLeon (Aunt Buckie)
Born 9 Dec 1909, Died 4 Mar 1975

Harold Tilton Buck

Frances Wellman (Gober) Sullivan (Aunt Tankie)
Born 8 Aug 1912, Died 19 Feb 1973

Frances Michael Sullivan
Born 30 Nov 1910, Died 11 Jan 1950

Harold Tilton (Scooter) Buck
Born 25 Nov 1936

Daniel Gober (Danny) Sullivan
Born 27 Oct 1938, Died 11 Oct 2011

Carol Joan (Sullivan) Kelly
Born 8 Nov 1943

CHAPTER ONE

IN THE BEGINNING

August 27, 1938—my big day—I get to come out into the world. My mother and father are so excited, especially Momma. She has been carrying me in her womb for over nine months, and the last four have been horrendous. You see, I was born in New Orleans, Louisiana, at Baptist Hospital on Napoleon Avenue. Can you imagine being pregnant without air-conditioning during all those long hot summer days in sultry New Orleans? On top of this, Mother gained forty pounds during her pregnancy. However, her tough life was just beginning because I remember her telling me how bad my colic was for months. They also talked about how I had to have casts on my legs and how they carried me around on a pillow! I'm not sure why.

Daddy, Momma, and me

Some interesting things that were also going on in 1938 were the following: Adolf Hitler was persecuting the Jews and started his move in Europe. Franklin D. Roosevelt was president during the Great Depression when the unemployment rate was at 19 percent. The minimum hourly wage was 40¢, the average house cost $3,900, and a gallon of gas only cost 10¢. Walt Disney released the classic film *Snow White and the Seven Dwarfs*.

Now let's get back to the main character. Charlotte, the name Momma and Daddy chose for me, was not my first name. They made it my middle name so my initials, ECG, would be the same as Daddy's. His name was Edgar Coleman Gober; my first name was Edith. Charlotte was chosen because Momma just liked it, but I was named Edith after my paternal grandmother, Edith Funk Gober. I was her first granddaughter. Momma was named Agnes Louise Echols, but Daddy thought it was Louise Agnes, and this is the way Daddy recorded it when she died. I didn't know this until I started the quest for my genealogy. However, let's get on with the story.

Momma and Daddy took me home to a small apartment at 920 Carrollton Avenue, Apartment K. Even though I don't remember much about this time in my life, I'm sure they were wonderful years because Momma and Daddy had been trying to have a baby since they got married on February 4, 1931. Daddy always told me that he wanted to get married on Valentine's Day, but Momma couldn't wait! (You might as well know now that my Daddy was a big teaser, and that is one of the many things I loved about him.) Momma was finally able to conceive after she had two operations to correct the position of her uterus.

Not very many people took photographs in the 1930s because they were expensive and complicated. However, here is one taken during my early years.

Momma, Daddy, and me (1939)

I must have known from the beginning that I was special and that my parents really loved me and wanted the best for me. Even then, they already knew how much I loved to hold, throw, pass, hit, catch, shoot, and drive a ball—any ball—and how I would continue to do so for the rest of my life! Life was good.

When I was five, Daddy took me to my second day at kindergarten, which I will never forget. We were driving next to a canal that ran beside the road. There were lots of open canals in New Orleans. I had to take my toothbrush, so I assume they were going to teach us how to brush our teeth.

I said, "Daddy, I really don't want to go to kindergarten."

Daddy said, "Then you don't have to go, and I'll just take you home." Home at this time, according to the 1940 Census, was 8116 Carrollton Avenue.

I'm really not sure of the conversation, but it was probably something like this because there's another thing you might as well know now—my father really spoiled me. Momma was in Atlanta at the time with a sick parent. You can bet I probably would have continued in kindergarten if Momma had been with Daddy and me that morning. She was the toughie, although you won't be able to tell if you look at the sweet picture that was taken of Momma and me on Easter Sunday 1942.

Easter at Lake Pontchartrain

The first home I can really recall was the one on Palmetto Street. It was a two-bedroom apartment with one bath, one living room, and one kitchen. By then, I had a little brother. Edgar "Eddie" Coleman Gober Jr. was born on September 9, 1941. He was three years younger than I, and we shared a bedroom. It is strange; I can still remember how our beds were placed in the room—very close with a window between us. Our two-story brick apartment building had four apartments—two on the top and two on the bottom. Ours was on the top floor.

We lived in the apartment from about 1943 until 1949, which was during World War II. One thing that really stands out in my mind was the gentleman who lived on the first floor opposite from our apartment. I don't remember his name, but I do remember his having these terrible coughing spells, which were caused by getting gassed while he was fighting in World War I, also known as the Great War. The war began in the summer of 1914, and those Germans finally surrendered late in 1918. The United States tried to remain neutral and therefore didn't even enter the war until early 1918. In those days, before television, neighbors would sit outside on the steps at night and talk to one another, so our neighbor's coughing attacks were easily heard throughout the neighborhood.

Donald Grasso and his Italian family lived across the hall from us. Even though they lived so close, we were never really good friends. Perhaps it was because he was not an athlete, or maybe it was because they were foreign to us and had a strange accent and even looked different. You see, he and his family had come all the way from New York. Since we didn't have many Italians in our neighborhood and they didn't act like us Southerners, we just thought them strange. I wouldn't say we were prejudiced, just from a different culture.

Some of my closest friends in the neighborhood were Mike and Gary Wilkerson. We played softball together with other kids in the apartments. This was so much fun; I loved sports of any kind at an early age. From the very beginning, I always did my very best and wanted to win, fair and square! The area where we played was a small quadrangle in front of Gary and Mike's apartment. Our home plate was in front of their apartment, and we tried to hit between the apartments on each side of our field. Unfortunately, this was not always accomplished, and we did have to replace quite a few windows. Also, I can remember playing toy soldiers with Gary and Mike. This was especially fun because we had someone's old Army helmet that we would fill up with water and bury in the ground to make a lake for our soldiers to maneuver around or through. One time, we even found a big turtle and had him swim in the helmet—what fun!

I guess part of the reason we liked playing toy soldiers was because of World War II that we were fighting in Europe. We were late entering the war because it wasn't our problem—that is, until the Japanese bombed Pearl Harbor on December 7, 1941. This was a terrible war with possibly 70 million fatalities; the Soviet Union was the big loser with 27 million. The Germans surrendered on May 8, 1945. But the Japanese didn't surrender until August 14, 1945, after we bombed Hiroshima and Nagasaki with atomic bombs. During most of the war, Franklin D. Roosevelt was our president. However, he died on April 12, 1945, and Harry S. Truman became president.

Daddy taught me to bowl when I was only six years old. He took me to Mid-City Bowling; it was at the intersection of Tulane and Carrollton Avenues. Eddie and I would go with Momma and Daddy many nights to the bowling alley. We would bowl while they played gin rummy with the owners, Jimmy and Claire Wittenberg. Eddie and I would rack our own bowling pins and bowl until late in the night, long after the bowling alley closed. However, when we bowled before it closed, there were some black pin boys who would set the pins for us. When you got through bowling, you'd just throw them whatever change you wanted. This was all the pay they received for their work. Today, we have automatic pinsetters and devices that even keep the score for you. However, I still like keeping my own score. It taught me to add really quickly in my head! The bowling alleys were where I first learned to gamble. There were slot machines all over the place, which was actually true throughout New Orleans, even in restaurants. New Orleans was kind of wild, and there was not a legal age, so Mother and Daddy didn't mind my playing any of the slots. Remember, this city had gambling casinos along with the Mafia influence. By the way, in the same little plaza with the bowling alley, there was a Katz and Besthoff drugstore where the soda fountain had the best hot fudge sundaes. Life was good.

At night, when our family went to bed, we would listen to the radio. Some of my favorite programs were *The Shadow*, *The Amos 'n' Andy Show*, *The Jack Benny Show*, *Inner Sanctum Mysteries*, *Blondie*, *The Lone Ranger*, *The Bob Hope Show*, *Fibber McGee and Molly*, and *The Life of Riley*, just to name a few. It was fun just lying there, many times with Daddy next to me in the dark and listening to these programs. *Inner Sanctum* and *The Shadow* were very scary, but all the others were funny.

Looking back, this was a happy, carefree time in my life. I did have to go to school, Judah P. Benjamin Elementary School, but this wasn't too bad. My teacher for first grade was Miss Mamoose. Would you believe she drew a great big moose on the blackboard? Yes, we had blackboards. Well, it must have worked because I can still remember her name. Daddy would take me on some days, but usually, I had to walk. We had only one car, and Daddy traveled from Monday through Thursday selling building materials for Tulane Hardwood Lumber Company. Actually, we were fortunate to have a car. Daddy's company was located right next to the bridge at Tulane and Carrollton Avenues, close to the bowling alley. Although the distance to school was a few miles, it wasn't that horrible because there were lots of us children walking together. No, we didn't have any blizzards to walk in. In fact, it didn't get too cold at all in New Orleans, but heat was another matter. As I got older, I rode my bike.

One unpleasant memory was when I got in the canal right across the street from our apartment. The walls were about twenty feet deep; however, it rarely had water more than a foot deep. It had three-foot concrete sides that went straight down and met the rest of the concrete that took a steep slope toward the bottom where the little stream was. Now I have to admit, Daddy had told me not to go into the canal, but I liked to go in there and take some chalk and draw big hearts showing who I loved that day. Well, I will never forget because Daddy—the one who always spoiled me and loved me so much—got me out of that canal, and did I ever get a whipping with his belt! I know now he was scared about my drowning because if we had a big flood, the canal could fill up quickly and I would be swept away into Lake Pontchartrain. However, at the time, it really hurt me in more ways than one.

I don't know if you have heard of chinaball trees, but there were some on the road that we took to school. They had beautiful violet blossoms that matured into our "ammunition." I loved climbing these trees. My friends and I made slingshots out of a tree branch and a piece of rubber tire. Boy, did we have some good fights. Those chinaberries really sailed, and they truly stung when you were on the other end of a shot.

During the time we lived in the apartment, I was going to the New Orleans Pelicans baseball games with my daddy. We could walk to the ballpark that was catercornered across the street from the bowling alley and close to Daddy's work. However, the path we took along the railroad tracks had hobo camps on each side, which were down a little lower than the tracks. The hobos also lived under the bridge by Daddy's office. Here I was carefree with my father, and there they were homeless, cooking over a campfire. I just took my blessings for granted back then but now realize how much I had, and I feel sorry for the hobos who had so little. They lived in tents and boxes and would jump on trains going from one city to the next. This was in the 1940s, not long after the Great Depression and during and after World War II. Daddy had gotten exempted from having to go to war because of his job and being married with two children.

Daddy had to travel all over the Southeast; and one time, I got to go with him to Mobile, Alabama. We stayed in the Cawthon Hotel, located right in downtown Mobile. I can remember the park right in front of the hotel where we fed the squirrels; it was a historical site called Bienville Square. Well, anyway, something happened on this trip that was not funny at the time. However, now I look back with fond memories because it was one of the special times I got to spend with Daddy. I always enjoyed being with him, but I did miss Momma—not for companionship, but for taking care of me. Daddy was the fun person; however, when we made this particular trip, I was only about six years old. He was not the best at doing my hair or taking care of my grooming. One morning, we got up, dressed, and went out into the hall to wait for the elevator. I was really looking forward to breakfast because Daddy always let me order whatever I wanted. All of a sudden, I screamed and ran for the room. This really scared Daddy as he's chasing behind me to see what was wrong. Can you believe—I forgot to put on my underwear!

For a six-year-old back in the 1940s, this was not funny. My father got to laugh and tell this story many times. Daddy has been dead for over thirty years; now I am glad I forgot my panties because he got so much enjoyment from telling this story through the years. I loved my wonderful father and his contagious laugh.

Something that seems strange now was the way the Catholic priests came right into our public school to teach catechism. We non-Catholics were allowed to walk to the Airline Baptist Church, which wasn't too far from school. This is where we received our Bible instruction from their teachers. This reminds me of the fact that we rarely went to church, except maybe on Easter, in order to show off the new dresses Momma and I bought. So until I became a Christian at twelve, that Baptist church was the only Christian instruction I received. However, when I was an infant, my momma and daddy had me christened at Saint Philip Cathedral in Atlanta in an area called Buckhead. This church was where my uncle Roddy (Roger Moise DeLeon) belonged and my two cousins Danny (Daniel Gober Sullivan) and Dodger (Roger Moise DeLeon Jr.)were also christened with me. I'll write more about these relatives later. This sounds like a snazzy church, and it is now, but then it was just an army barracks.

The three cousins' christening
Granddaddy Dan Gober, Grandmother Edith, Aunt Buckie
holding Danny; Dodger is the baby on the left side at front,
and I'm on the right side at front. Sorry, I don't know
the other two ladies or the gentleman on far right!

Most days, I would hurry home from school in time for Mr. Delaney's arrival (can you believe I still remember his name after sixty years?). He would come every day in his truck with a section in the back that lifted up and held the snowball machine along with all these wonderful bottles filled with sugary syrup. I have always had a problem with sugar, and my excitement started at a young age. My, my, so many colorful flavors to choose from, but I always got vanilla and chocolate mixed—delicious! How excited I was by just the sound of the music coming from his truck to announce his arrival and draw all his customers. Momma always gave me a nickel to make the purchase. Life was good.

While we were still living in the apartment, I got to go to an Easter egg hunt at a house where some of the Mafia lived. Until now, I believe that I went to Frank Costello's house in Metairie, but I'm not so sure which Mafia member it was. According to a site on the Internet, Costello was from New York and Carlos Marcello was the godfather of the Mafia in New Orleans. The site also wrote about the beginning of the Mafia in New Orleans in 1934, when they brought the slot machines with the help of the then senator Huey P. Long. By the end of 1947, Marcello was in charge of the most important gambling casinos in New Orleans. He lived a life of crime and was even rumored to have been involved with the assassination of the Kennedy brothers. Marcello died in Metairie in 1993. At the time, the only name I heard was Costello, and my daddy was the one who was familiar with this element of society. Yes, he did go to the gambling houses. If I were betting, I bet it was Marcello's home, and Costello was in the business with him and may have been there.

Now you are probably wondering how this little fifth grader got invited to some member of the Mafia's house. Well, I had a friend named Stephanie, and she lived with her poor divorced mother in one of the apartments that enclosed the quadrangle where we played ball. She invited me to go to her uncle's house for this egg hunt. Notice I said "poor divorced mother." Well, I expressed it this way because nobody's mother was divorced back then, or so it seemed. Their house in Metairie was a large two-story with a well-manicured lawn. It was probably the most beautiful house in which I had ever been. There were lots of people, and I was really excited. It's hard to recall what they looked like, but I can remember the men were dressed up in suits and the women had lovely dresses. Back then, everyone dressed up. They got us all together and told us whoever found the raw egg would win the grand prize. They wished us "Good hunting" and turned us loose. Well, I have to admit I watched the lady of the house and noticed she kept watching a particular area whenever a child would get close to it. Yes, I went over and really did a thorough hunt in that area, and—lo and behold—there was the white raw egg that would win that great big chocolate egg. Lucky me. And surprise! Inside the big chocolate egg were cookies. Life was good.

I wish I could end each chapter with "Life was good"; however, life was not always good. One day, when I was about nine, I went to City Park for an end-of-school outing. I was playing in one of the beautiful gigantic oak trees with big branches covered with Spanish moss. Many of the branches draped down and met the ground. Well, lo and behold, I looked up; and on one of these branches, there was this man calling me to come up where he was! I was so scared because I could see him with his pants down, playing with himself. I ran to my teacher, who reported the incident to the police. Back then, this was such a big deal that a detective came to my house trying to investigate the case. They never did catch him, as far as I know.

CHAPTER TWO

GROWING UP IN METAIRIE

We lived in the apartment until I went into the sixth grade. Then we moved to Metairie and lived at 14 Brockenbraugh Court, just off Metairie Road. We rented a house that was much nicer than our apartment. It had two bedrooms, two bathrooms, and a large living room with a big kitchen. Upstairs, there was a big bonus room that ran the length of the house, and there was a detached garage. Along with this great house, we had a large yard with huge pecan trees; our living environment had greatly improved from the little apartment. Daddy rented this house from Vernon "Lefty" Haynes for two years. Coach Haynes would be my geometry teacher, and he also coached the boys' basketball team at Metairie High School. Years later, in 1988, I visited New Orleans to attend the Republican National Convention as an alternate delegate. I went out to see the house and all of my old surroundings. I was surprised to see that Metairie High School had been renamed Vernon C. Haynes Middle School. I was curious to know how this happened and learned that, in 1912, Metairie had been a one-room schoolhouse with fifty-four students. In 1929, a large two-story brick building was built, and this was the way it looked when I went there. When I left in 1955, several schools in Jefferson Parish combined into East Jefferson Consolidated School, and Metairie High School became Metairie Middle School; Mr. Haynes became principal. In November 1974, they tore down the old building; the new structure was named Vernon C. Haynes Middle School in honor of the former principal, distinguished educator, and my long-ago landlord and teacher.

We really enjoyed living in this house. It had an old dilapidated basketball goal in the backyard, without a net on the hoop, where Daddy taught me to play basketball. In the garage, Daddy put a piece of plywood on top of two wooden horses, added a net, and taught me to play Ping-Pong. As you can already tell, Daddy really enjoyed my athleticism and encouraged me to play many sports. I don't know who enjoyed my athletic accomplishments more, Daddy or me! There was a vacant lot just a couple of doors down from our house where I played a lot of tackle football with the boys. Now I wish I had not played—although I really liked it—because by the time I was twelve, I had knee problems. These knees have interfered with my activities intermittently throughout my life.

My momma was a good cook and homemaker. We ate a lot of meat and potatoes, and Eddie and I had to clean our plates. However, lots of times, Eddie would feed his to Tiny, our pet dog, when Momma wasn't looking. Daddy traveled at least four days a week. But on weekends, he would squeeze fresh orange juice; and on Sunday nights, he would make us little sandwiches out of peanut butter on Ritz Crackers with a slice of banana on top. Even today, I absolutely love peanut butter and banana! It is like my comfort food. Momma was not big on desserts but would make a wonderful banana pudding and also some chocolate pudding. Other than these desserts, she would buy seven-layer chocolate cakes and apple pies from Maison Blanche, a downtown department store on Canal Street. On the other hand, she really wanted us to be healthy; and along with our big breakfasts of eggs, bacon, oatmeal, and toast, she made sure we had our cod-liver oil—ugh!

When we moved to Metairie, besides the wonderful house and yard, I also had to attend a new school and make new friends. My best friend was Adrienne Maitre. She and her family played a big role in my life for three years. When I started to attend Metairie High School, I thought it had twelve grades, but this was not the case. It had all the grades from first to twelfth except for the eighth; I had to go to Metairie Grammar School for that grade because the high school was too crowded.

On the first day, there were two classes for sixth graders; they put me in a class with Mr. Alvin Bertaut. Now he was a good-looking young man with big muscles. In fact, he later became Mr. New Orleans. However, I did not want to be in his class because he scared me; I had always had lady teachers. Fortunately, the administration listened to my pleas and put me in Miss Anita Weilbacher's class; I was so grateful. She was very kind, and I can remember how she would make us put our heads down on our desks after lunch while she read *Little Women* to us. She was an *old maid*, and we got along so well; I would even go to her house to wrestle with her Doberman pinscher. She is one of the teachers who really encouraged me. I'll never forget her; I can still see the twinkle in her blue eyes when she smiled.

During the two years we lived in the Haynes house, besides playing football, Ping-Pong, bowling, and basketball, I had my first boyfriend, Tu-Tu Nugent. He was a really cool guy, even though he did have a lot of freckles. Tu-Tu was so strong that he actually rode around with me on the crossbar of his bike, which put us pretty close.

One year, we had a Halloween party upstairs in our attic. As part of the party activities, we all went trick-or-treating on our street. We were having a great time until something very traumatic occurred. My friend from school, Billy Johnson, went up three steps to this house and rang the doorbell. All of a sudden, the door flew open, and this guy about thirty years old didn't say a word; he just socked Billy right in the face. We had to take Billy back to our house and treat his cut lip—not a good party. It seems weird now, but we never sued or got the police to investigate this guy's behavior—another sign of the times.

I have always loved my pets. When I was little, we had a Boston bulldog named Tiny. I'm not sure what happened to this dog, but I did have my picture taken with him. Unfortunately, when we lived in the apartment, we weren't allowed to have a pet. After we moved into the Haynes house, we got Tiny Two. This was a really high-strung toy fox terrier that only liked to eat cooked chicken. We kept Tiny Two until she died of a nervous breakdown when she was about ten. I guess it's hard to think of a dog having a nervous breakdown, but Tiny Two was very nervous; and I can still see her, in her chair in Momma and Daddy's bedroom, shivering and looking so fragile in the warmth of her blanket.

I wanted another pet. I don't remember whatever possessed me to want a chicken and a fully grown one at that. One day, I took money I had saved up (I did get an allowance) and rode my bike about five miles to a butcher shop that sold chickens. I bought a Rhode Island Red hen. I can remember riding home, holding my chicken's legs to the handlebars, making it without a wreck. I loved my chicken; she would follow me around the yard and was really fun. One day, I forgot to put her back in her cage, and one of the bad dogs from the neighborhood came over and killed her. I was very sad.

Adrienne and I were in the same class until she went to an exclusive private school. We had so much fun. I would spend the night over at her house; since she was an only child, we didn't have to put up with the likes of Eddie. One summer, her mother, Grace, taught Adrienne and me how to sew. She had an old White sewing machine that would only go in one direction and do straight stitches. That was enough for her to teach us to make a skirt. Later, Momma bought that machine from Mrs. Maitre for $5. Even though I was not the best seamstress in the world, it saved me so much money. Years later, after I got married, I was able to make many of my maternity clothes and tennis outfits on that machine. Adrienne and I enjoyed playing all the sports that I had grown to love. We were always with the boys because they liked to play sports as well. However, I'm sure that wasn't the only reason they came around because Adrienne was quite the beauty. She was also intelligent, petite, and fun-loving; and she matured before most of the other girls, including me, which explains why the boys loved being around her. One day, Adrienne and I bleached a small strip of our bangs with peroxide.

Boy, did we look sexy. Mrs. Maitre was a fun person, and she even played Ping-Pong with us in their garage. She and Momma became best friends as well, even though I believe they were so different; Momma didn't play sports, and Mrs. Maitre was so *cool*, while my momma was serious. Momma seemed much older than Mrs. Maitre, but I recently asked Adrienne her momma's birth date, and it was February 4, 1911. Wow, Momma was born on August 14, 1910, so Mrs. Maitre was almost as old as Momma! The other neat thing—Grace was born on the same day and month of Momma and Daddy's wedding day. Surely they discovered that along the way.

One summer, Mr. and Mrs. Maitre invited me to go to Panama City Beach with them. This turned out to be one of the most memorable times of my life. Since I had grown up in New Orleans, I was used to hurricanes; they were really exciting to me. Why, in the old apartment, we all gathered for the hurricane parties. All the neighbors brought food to share, including delicious desserts. We played games and ate. Besides all this entertainment, the wind was so strong it would blow the water through the sides of the windows, and we would watch the water trickle down the walls. What fun times and so exciting! Later, when all the rain and wind stopped, we would go outside our building and watch the boats going by in the floodwaters. Evidently, the canal couldn't get the water out fast enough; and when it was filled all the way to the top, I could touch the canal water. Anyway, it was a pretty thrilling time for me as a kid.

However, Mr. Maitre did not share this view of hurricanes. We had not been on the Gulf Coast very long when Mr. Maitre heard something about a hurricane. I might as well tell you—one of my pet peeves is when people call this area the "ocean," and oh, that just drives me crazy—it is the *Gulf* Coast. Well, anyway, in 1951, we didn't get much warning when the hurricanes were coming; and all of a sudden, Mr. Maitre was packing us up to dash off in his green Cadillac. His aim was to go inland and escape being hit by the hurricane that was heading right where we were. Adrienne and I were so upset. Can you imagine—leaving the coast and going inland? Well, of course, who was going to listen to us? So off we went! Mr. Maitre was driving fast, going somewhere inland; he didn't care where. Just get him away from the gulf! Finally, he decided to stop at a small motel and get us a room. This was not a good thing for Mr. Maitre because, by now, Adrienne and I were so excited, along with their dog (would you believe named Stormy!) that was not supposed to be with us. All we wanted to do was jump on the beds and wait for the hurricane to arrive. What a night! We finally got to sleep with the clamoring sounds of the wind and rain beating against the windows. It's a wonder that poor Mr. Maitre didn't have a heart attack. He survived, and the next day was calm; he drove us back to Panama City Beach, Florida, for a few more days of fun on the beach. Just one little problem—the room where we had been before the hurricane was damaged; the sand eroded under it. Don't worry, we found another room and had our fun vacation. Life was good.

God used this quiet, serious man as an instrument in my becoming a Christian. I mentioned earlier that my family didn't go to church; however, they were neither atheists nor agnostics. They just didn't go to church. Well, Mr. Maitre invited me to go to

Munholland Memorial Methodist Church one Sunday with Adrienne and him. Mrs. Maitre was Catholic and did not go to church. Even though I had not been encouraged by Mother and Daddy to become a Christian, I had always desired to know Him. I'm not sure why. Perhaps it was the exposure I had at the Baptist church; the prayers of my maternal grandmother, Carrie Strickland Echols; the times I went to Christmas candlelight services with my Uncle Roddy; or perhaps the longing in the soul for something to fill it. When I visited the church, Adrienne and I decided to take the confirmation classes they offered and be baptized together on Easter Sunday, March 25, 1951. This was a very special day for me because I accepted Christ as my Savior. I remember that my family came and seemed pleased that I had made this commitment. Since then, I have always wanted to know Jesus and His will for my life. I guess the reason that Momma was pleased for me was because even though she was not very spiritual, her mother, Carrie, was. Both of my parents often talked about Grandmother Carrie and how she really loved the Lord. They said her preacher would come over and they would discuss the Bible. I really know from what Momma and Daddy said that Grandmother had a personal relationship with Him.

Until eighth grade, Momma enrolled me in dance lessons. I had to do ballet, tap, and acrobatics. Of course, I liked acrobatics best and would go early in order to do tumbling with my friend Anne Cunningham out on the lawn in front of my instructor's house. I was the strong one who would throw her around, and she would do flips while I was on the ground holding her up. What fun! Actually the ballet and tap weren't too bad either. During my dance career, I gave Daddy another good story to talk and laugh about for years. It happened when I was about twelve; we had our dance recital in the auditorium at Metairie High School. I had a solo role in the recital. I was to be the prince, probably because I was the tallest girl in our dance studio at five feet, eight inches tall, and they needed a big prince. I had this costume that included a black leotard, black tights, and also this cute frilly tutu. My little dance went in a circle, and I would go, "One, two, three, leap." I was trying so hard. "One, two, three, leap. One, two, three, leap—" Uh-oh! I took a giant leap right into the floodlights and fell down. I can't remember dancing anymore after that. I had taken dance for about five years, and amazingly, I am really glad Momma wanted me to be more feminine and graceful. She tried to offset Daddy's sports influence. She did not want me to be such a jock. However, I believe that the dance was really good for my coordination and made me a better athlete.

Although I was athletic, I told you Momma was trying to make sure that I remembered I was a girl. She also wanted me to have beautiful teeth, so I wore braces when I was twelve. My teeth were not crooked, but I had lost my eyetooth—no no, not from sports or a fight with Eddie! But when my permanent teeth came in, the two eyeteeth were little peg teeth. No one knew where I inherited these little teeth, but anyway, when I was about ten, one of them got abscessed from a piece of popcorn going up under the gum. I went into the hospital where they removed the tooth, leaving a gap. Later, I only wore the braces for nine months because my teeth had shifted and filled in the place for the tooth I lost. After the braces, they gave me a little flipper tooth to fill in the gap and got the other peg tooth capped. This cap is still looking great to this day. My daddy told me not to let them attach a permanent tooth to my other teeth because he had one that abscessed just like that. I used this flipper tooth until I was in my sixties; then I got an implant—wish I never had!

Momma was always trying to make me beautiful. Besides trying to straighten out my teeth, she always tried to keep my naturally straight hair—curly. Momma made sure that it stayed curly by giving my permanents. Oh, they were so bad back then. They would attach you to some strange-looking machine that had a wire going down to each one of the chemical-wrapped curlers that would heat the hair and curl it for maybe weeks. This is when stores called "beauty shops" began to open, offering haircuts, styling, and giving these permanent waves. The beauty shops created places for women to gather and socialize while their hair was done. Momma was very attractive and she wanted me to look the same. Momma made sure I shaved my legs and wore pretty dresses. Honestly, I also liked to look pretty as long as it didn't interfere with my sports. One thing Momma couldn't fix were my pitiful nails. If the nail or the cuticle got dry or raggedy, I just had to bite them and still do! Momma had the most beautiful well-manicured long nails, and I had a big problem with mine!

All my sex education also began while we lived in the Haynes house. I can still see Momma and Daddy making love in their bedroom when I walked in on them; I thought Daddy was hurting Momma. I was so upset, but they tried to calm me down. The next day after I caught them, Momma took me to Maison Blanche. She told me to wait for her a few feet away in the book department while she bought me a book. Big deal, the name of the book was *Growing Up* and it showed pictures of animals with their babies. Years later, I saw a copy of this same book at a garage sale in Atlanta. It was not an in-depth sex education book!

Someone that I haven't talked about much was my brother, Eddie. Just thinking about his life breaks my heart and makes me sad. I might as well get this over with now.

CHAPTER THREE

MY BROTHER EDDIE

When he was a little guy, we called him Eddie Boy. He was a cute little white-headed kid with blue eyes. Somehow, Eddie was different even at an early age. He seemed very shy, and I know it was hard for him to grow up in the shadow of his outgoing sister. As I have mentioned on many occasions in my story, Daddy and I had a great relationship. He and I both enjoyed sports, playing cards, and board games. We were both math people. It seems as if Eddie tried to play sports and he was athletic, but never really enjoyed the discipline or whatever it took to continue playing.

Momma, Daddy, Eddie, and me (1952)

He had problems with school from the beginning. Since Eddie had a September birthday, he was not quite four when he began kindergarten. He was also a momma's boy and really didn't like to leave her. Years later, Momma said she wished she had not sent him to school until the year he was to turn seven.

I know he repeated the third grade and never completed high school. Momma was always going to school for conferences. I remember many mornings when Eddie took his temperature to show Momma that he really was too sick to go to school. I know Momma took him to a psychiatrist and they said he was having some kind of mental problem. I believe they said he was schizophrenic. He started using drugs at twelve and that certainly didn't help.

Eddie and I would have some terrible fights; I was always bigger and stronger, so he had a rough time. The main defense he used was pulling my hair, and unfortunately for me, my hair was long and easy to grab. Boy, did that hurt! This reminds me of a terrible thing I did in the rented house on Brockenbraugh Court in Metairie. One day, I was babysitting Eddie, and I can still remember being in Momma and Daddy's bedroom when I told him to do something and he just wouldn't. So I got my BB gun out and pointed it at his stomach, and I said, "You better do what I told you or else I am going to shoot you." He didn't, and I did. It scared the fire out of me. He didn't have a shirt on, but fortunately, it didn't break the skin. I am very sorry and embarrassed now, to think I so lost it that I would shoot my brother.

I don't remember being punished, but I know I never did anything like that again. I recall that when he was twelve, he got a motor scooter that he and his best friend, Albert Blalock, would ride around E. William David Parkway and our whole neighborhood. This is when he began drinking and using drugs. He was out of control. Later, after we moved to Chamblee, Georgia, I can remember his hurting Momma. He had her down in the hallway by the laundry closet when I came in and pulled him off her. He was about fourteen.

When Eddie turned seventeen, he got Mother and Daddy to sign a paper so he could go into the navy. This was another big mistake. Eddie ended up going overseas to Korea. When he came home, he said, "I could buy a girl for a pack of cigarettes." He was able to get all kinds of drugs overseas. After he returned to the United States, he went AWOL. It was just close to two years of his four-year commitment. He went to stay with his girlfriend, Louise. Eddie never knew that my father told the authorities where he was, and they got him. He received a general discharge because of medical (mental) problems.

He married Louise in 1961. They had three children—Charles Perry, born July 1, 1963; Sheila, born November 7, 1964; and Sheryl, born November 8, 1976. He continued doing his drugs. One time, he even got arrested for growing marijuana in his yard. Momma and Daddy built a house for him next to theirs in Norcross, attached to Grandmother's farm. This was fortunate for his son Chuck, as Charles Perry was called, and his sister Sheila because Momma and Daddy were there for them. Sheryl was not born until after Momma and Daddy died, so Eddie had a lot more influence on her life because she spent much of her time at home alone with him. Eddie had four grandchildren—Sheila's son, Scott Lee Shelton, born

January 8, 1982; Sheryl's daughter, Morgan Folse, born March 24, 1997; Chuck's daughter, Jamie, born June 10, 1994; and Chuck's son, Jayson, born May 16, 1997.

Picture I gave Momma in 1972 of her
grandchildren—Ken, Lane, Chuck, and Sheila

One time, after Mother and Daddy died, my Aunt Kappy (Kathryn Echols Crawford) and I had Eddie committed to Georgia Regional Hospital for observation. They kept him, gave him haloperidol (Haldol), and then released him. The medicine really zonked him; he was so pitiful, and I felt so sad for him. He was able to draw disability due to his mental problems and ended up selling everything and moving into a little apartment by himself.

Even though he was living alone in the apartment, Louise never divorced him, although he was not a good husband. She would go over and make sure his needs were met. One day, he fell and broke his hip. They took him to the hospital, and all I know is that he was cussing the nurses out. He had to have surgery. Unfortunately, there were complications and he died shortly after the surgery. His death was due in part to his nicotine addiction; his arteries were restricted. The doctors wanted to give him something to help the blood flow, but he had told them he didn't want them to give him anything to prevent his death, so he died. It was April 16 2001; he was only fifty-nine years old.

He had inherited the two burial lot next to Momma and Daddy; however, Eddie had sold his cemetery lots to his son, Chuck. This is one of many examples of how my brother was not normal. He sold these lots in order to buy a refrigerator to hold cigarettes. He never wanted to run out of these killers. My brother Eddie was cremated and his ashes were put into a jar. His wife, Louise, has kept them all these years.

CHAPTER FOUR

SUMMER FUN IN NORCROSS, GEORGIA

Of course, some of my fondest memories were the times that I spent in Norcross, Georgia, with my father's eldest sister, Eugenia DeLeon. Eugenia sounds so strange because everyone called her John; I called her Aunt John. She was married to Uncle Roddy, and their son was my cousin Dodger. Not that it matters, but Dodger was twenty-two days older than I since he was born on August 5, 1938. Actually, it did matter to me! He was always the older cousin, which when we were young, was good for him; but in recent years, it has been good for me because he is always the old one.

Our family would go to Norcross every Christmas, and I would visit every summer. Almost as soon as school was out for the summer vacation, I would ride the Southerner train from New Orleans to Atlanta by myself. I started traveling alone from the time I was six years old. I loved going to my Aunt John's and the nine-acre farm that was shared with my grandmother, Edith. Grandmother lived there with her three dogs and lots of cats. Some summers, she had forty—yes, this is not a typo—forty!

When I arrived in Atlanta to spend the summers, I can remember Grandmother, Aunt John, Uncle Roddy, and Dodger all meeting me at the old Union Station in downtown Atlanta. It was built in 1930 between Forsyth and Spring Streets. I had been on the train from eight o'clock that morning until seven o'clock that night and was really hungry. So we would head for the Varsity as soon as I got off the train. The Varsity was a famous drive-in restaurant on North Avenue that opened in 1928; by 1950, it had one hundred black carhops and was the largest drive-in restaurant in the world. Those carhops would jump on the back of your car as soon as you entered the parking lot. It was really exciting to see them fight for our car. Would you believe, in 1939, Clark Gable ate there when he was in Atlanta for the world premiere of *Gone with the Wind*? Besides all this, Dodger and I could really put away the hamburgers which were only 15¢ back in the 1940s. Don't forget the "naked dogs" (you know, a hot dog without any condiments), french fries, apple pies, PCs (plain chocolate milk with crushed ice, of course), and frosted oranges (an orange drink that was blended with a scoop of vanilla ice cream). Yum-yum. Life was good.

All through the summers, I had the opportunity to spend lots of time with Grandmother. I did call her Grandmother, not like Dodger and the other four grandchildren, who called her Ancient! I'm not sure when they started calling her Ancient, but she did outlive three of her four children, dying at the age of eighty-nine. How blessed I was to get to spend my summers on the farm; Grandmother had ducks, goats, turkeys, pigs, chickens, rabbits, cows, and horses, in addition to the dogs and cats.

With all of these animals, Grandmother was grateful for the help of Henry Denson, a black man whom Grandmother took in as a young boy. Of course, slavery had long since been abolished, but he did depend on Grandmother to provide for him until he got married and got his own place. Henry used to squirt warm milk right into my mouth while he was milking the cows, then he would give me a big smile with his gold front tooth just shining. He was also really good at ringing the necks of the chickens and then taking the feathers off before they were cooked and eaten. This is where I certainly learned to understand the phrase "running around like a chicken without a head"! Henry got the turkeys dressed for market as well. Grandmother sold the turkeys at Thanksgiving and Christmas to all of Aunt John's patients in the rich area of Buckhead. We'd deliver them in Grandmother's big black Buick.

A special time for Grandmother and me was when we would sit out on her concrete back porch and pick fleas off the scrawny cats and kittens. There had been a lot of inbreeding! Close to the porch, Grandmother also had a springhouse, a place where she kept things cool in the stream that ran through the twelve-by-twelve-foot building. Well, of course, while we picked fleas, we talked a lot, right beside the bubbling creek where the water moccasins and tadpoles lived. However, the cats didn't seem to appreciate these special times as we chased each one down for its turn in our laps.

I guess you are wondering where my grandfather was. Well, his name was Daniel Gober; people called him Dan. He was born on June 19, 1883, in Pitts Point, Kentucky. He died on May 1, 1951, just before my thirteenth birthday, so I don't remember much about him. He had a really bad temper and would cuss out animals as well as people. Granddaddy had diabetes; I do recall Granddaddy seemed to always have some delicious hard candy sticks that he would give me. A brain tumor took his life in spite of the wonderful care that my Aunt John got for him at Emory University Hospital. Aunt John knew the doctors, and she made sure he had the best care possible. Something I never figured out about Granddaddy was the fact that he had graduated from the medical school at Centre College in Kentucky, but chose to go into the insurance business. He was about five feet, ten inches tall and weighed about two hundred pounds. I was always told that Grandmother loved her life on Club Drive in Brookhaven; however, Granddaddy moved her out to the country in Norcross. The Gober clan was Dan, Edith, Eugenia (Aunt John), Coleman (Daddy), Catherine (Aunt Buckie), and Frances (Aunt Tankie).

Happy days when Aunt John and
Roger "Uncle Roddy" DeLeon got married
L-R: Edith, Coleman, Frances, Roger, Eugenia, Catherine, and Dan

One summer, Grandmother gave me a kitten to take home on the train in a cardboard box. That was not a good thing—uh-oh! About halfway home, the kitten went to the bathroom in his box; and some way or another, he got out, and I had to chase it all over the car. However, I did manage to get my kitty, Tom, home, where he lived a long and happy life.

Besides having my cousins to play with, I also had some good friends in Norcross. Two special ones lived right up the road from us, Tommy and Sylvia Cape. In fact, I really loved Tommy. He didn't love me though. I say this because I can still remember his having a birthday party one year on July 2, and we played spin the bottle. When it was my turn to spin, it pointed at Tommy. Well, he was supposed to give me a kiss, but he got up and ran out of the house. Don't worry though; I chased him and tackled him as he got caught in the privet hedges close to his house. I hate to tell you—this did not win his affections, although I got my kiss.

As I have mentioned, there was a creek with water moccasins down by Grandmother's house, but they never bothered us. In an area close to the creek, Grandmother had beautiful blue hydrangeas and gardenia bushes growing in her yard. The shrubs had beautiful blossoms on them, and I can remember using them when burying some dead animals, like a bird or squirrel. I placed the beautiful frothy blue blossoms in the hole and made a pretty little place to put the animal to rest. Years later, I transplanted some of the hydrangeas to my yard. It's always a special blessing when I have those beautiful blooms to remind me of those wonderful days with Grandmother.

Dodger had a motor scooter, and we would ride all over Norcross. We were only about twelve years old when Dodger got the scooter. Norcross-Tucker Road was a dirt road. In those days, everybody knew everybody, and Sheriff Grady Simpson didn't worry about our riding around without a helmet or license. However, one day, I did melt some skin on the inside of my calf on Dodger's hot exhaust pipe. I had a scar there for many years. Besides the dirt roads, no helmets, no license, and everybody knowing everybody, the phone system was very different. When we used the phone, we would pick it up and turn the crank that rang the operator. We would talk to her, and she knew who we were. We told her who we wanted or gave her the four-digit number, and there they were! Dodger's number was 2664; I guess I remember it because here it is, 2010, and Dodger still has the same number—well, almost the same. Through the years, they gave him 448-2664, and then as Atlanta grew, they added area codes, so Dodger's number is now 770-448-2664—a far cry from when life was so simple. We also had party lines, and you had to know your ring so you would know whether or not the call was for you.

I can remember Auntie Maud Rogers also; she could really cook and was always so nice to us. She didn't live with us, but was there about every day, cooking, cleaning, and helping Grandmother. I know a lot of people, especially Yankees, believe that all Southerners mistreated black people, but I can say we really loved Auntie Maud and Henry. We treated them like family. That's not to say that slavery was not a terrible thing. My grandmother's family had owned slaves in Kentucky, but I never asked her how she felt about it. I'm not sure whose biscuits were the best, Grandmother's or Auntie Maud's, but I tell you, Dodger and I and some other family members had many a good breakfast throwing the biscuits to one another around Grandmother's pine-paneled dining room. This is the room where Grandmother would give us a time-out whenever we misbehaved.

While we are talking about the relations between blacks and whites, I want you to know that, in the South, there were those who were prejudiced, and my father was one of them. Fortunately, I did not agree with him on this account. However, I never went to school with any black children. In fact, it's probably hard for you to imagine that when I rode the streetcars in New Orleans on Canal Street, blacks were not allowed to sit in the front. Therefore, when we reached the end of the line, blacks would have to get up, go out, and walk around to the back of the car. Also, they were not allowed to drink from the same water fountain as whites, nor could they go to our schools, theaters, or churches. This was called segregation. It was not until 1955, when Rosa Parks refused to give up her seat on a bus in Montgomery, Alabama, to a white person that a lot of ruckus started. This was after the Supreme Court ruled in 1954, in the *Brown v. Board of Education* case in Topeka, Kansas, that segregation of the schools was unconstitutional. In 1957, nine black students in Arkansas entered Little Rock Central High School. This was a real battle and the next year the school board closed all the public schools rather than integrate. It was not until 1972 that all the public schools were integrated. Sorry about this digression, but I wanted you all to realize that this is the way it was when I grew up.

After we moved to Atlanta, my mother had a maid, Ella Mae Westbrook. I "inherited" her after Momma died, and I can still remember her saying, "Yes, ma'am" to me, even though I was thirty years younger. Ella worked many years for me until she retired. She and her husband, Charlie, put their children, Vernon and Sandra, through college. When Ella died, Sandra called me, and I attended her funeral. She was a very special Christian lady who blessed my life. Okay, back to the farm!

One summer, I can remember taking a sled up on the hill by Grandmother's house. (Years later, on the top of this area, they cut a boulevard right through it named after Jimmy Carter.) Dodger had the sled for "all" the Georgia snow, but I didn't get to see much snow during the winters in New Orleans, so to go sledding was a treat for me. Only problem was, we did this in the summers. We would take the sled up on the hill and head down toward the creek; the pine needles made for a really fast ride. We had to be sure to hit a tree to stop us from going over the bank and dropping six feet into the creek. Well, you guessed it; I missed the tree, went over the cliff into the creek, and broke my wrist. I took it easy after that and just played cards a lot that summer. Oh, we loved to play canasta and poker.

Another summer, my Aunt Tankie taught me to play bridge. Thanks to Aunt Tankie, I have enjoyed this game throughout my life. Oh yeah, you are probably wondering where she came from; well, she was my father's baby sister who moved into Aunt John's garage apartment. Aunt Tankie was another one with a nickname, but her real name was Frances. She and her two children, Danny and Joan, came up from Pompano Beach, Florida, in 1952, when her husband, Dr. Francis "Sully" Sullivan, died of cirrhosis of the liver.

In 1954, another of Grandmother's children moved from Pompano Beach to the farm—my Aunt Buckie (Edith Katherine Buck) and her husband, Harold Tilton Buck. They remodeled Grandmother's barn into a really unique house. My cousin Scooter, whose real name was Harold Tilton Buck III, came with them after he graduated from high school. Scooter, born on November 23, 1936, was our eldest cousin; Dodger, next; then me; Danny (two months younger than I); Eddie; and last, Joan. After Tankie and Buckie moved to the farm, three of Grandmother's four children were there. Daddy finally moved up to Atlanta in 1955 and later built a house next to the farm in 1961. Oh, wait! I'm getting ahead of myself.

One day, my cousin Scooter took all of us young cousins for a ride. Wow, you won't believe what we saw. There was a huge dam being built to make a gigantic lake called Lake Lanier, named for Sidney Lanier. I remember being high up and looking down on one of the valleys getting filled up with water from the Chattahoochee River. There were houses and farmlands disappearing. This project began in 1950, and the lake was finally full in May of 1959. It was in the summer of 1954 that we took our little trip up to Buford with Scooter, who, by the way, drank beer. He was our eldest and wildest cousin.

My Aunt John worked in Atlanta for—Dr. Tommy Atkins and later Dr. Ralph Murphy. Many of the affluent people in Atlanta, including a lot of the Coca-Cola executives, were their patients. They would call my Aunt John—Dr. Johnny. She was the only one of Grandmother's children who even went to college. My Aunt John wanted to be a doctor. She was a member of Agnes Scott's

Phi Beta Kappa Society that was founded in 1776. She then went to Yale School of Medicine when very few females were permitted to attend. However, something went wrong with an experiment in the science lab and her lungs got fumes in them; she came home and never went back. The funny thing is, as smart as John was, she never learned to drive a car.

On Saturdays, I would go to work with her on the Greyhound bus from Norcross to the W. W. Orr Doctors Building. This building, at 478 Peachtree Street, was built in 1930. It was the second high-rise in Atlanta with eleven stories. I loved going to work with Aunt John. One thing she would do was prick my finger to check my blood and then rave about how great it was. We would work until noon, then Grandmother would pick us up and we'd go grocery shopping at Happy Herman's. After shopping, we might get to eat at Twelve Oaks or the Colonnade Restaurant on Cheshire Bridge Road. Wow! Sometimes we would go swimming at Mooney's Lake on Morosgo Drive, close to what is now Sidney Marcus Boulevard. Aunt John loved her gardening, so we would stop by Hastings Nature & Garden Center after Herman's. I believe I got my love for gardening not only from my mother, but also from Aunt John. Life was good.

My story would not be complete if I didn't describe this woman who influenced my life so much. Even though, as I have mentioned, Aunt John was well educated and brilliant—when she was home on the farm, she was a sight. I told you she liked to garden, and I can still see her out in the yard in her cotton housedress that was worn so thin that one of her great big breasts had ripped a slit in it, showing part of her boob hanging out. She would not wear any underwear while working in the yard; therefore, she never had to go into the house and interrupt her work for such things as going to the bathroom!

Aunt John and Ken with Grandmother Edith
in the background (Easter 1963)
Must have been her best housedress since it was Easter!

Her yard was so beautiful, and so was her house. We had to take our shoes off at the back door. She had a collection of the most beautiful goblets that she displayed by the fireplace in the great room. Uncle Roddy would always mop the big room for her, but John did everything else, including cooking. Boy, could she cook. Our night meal was a feast, perhaps because Aunt John worked so hard during the day that she only ate dinner. However, even though she only ate one meal, Aunt John was heavy—I hate to say fat. This is part of the reason why she lived to be only sixty years old. Probably the bigger reason was the fact that she smoked Chesterfield cigarettes and she didn't get much sleep. I can also remember one of their dogs, Missy Moe, a black cocker spaniel. Whenever I trip over something, I often think of how Uncle Roddy used to get on my case and call me the clumsiest girl he had ever seen—just because I would step into Missy Moe's water bowl and turn it over—quite frequently! But remember, these kinds of remarks never got me down. Thanks to Daddy, whenever people teased me, it was because they loved me and I was special. Besides, I couldn't help that I wore a size nine shoe at the time, and Missy's water bowl was right there next to the kitchen door! By the way, after I had two children, my foot grew to eleven and a half slim! I always felt loved by my special Aunt John, and I know that, in so many ways, she influenced my life.

The big event on the farm, in 1950, was when Aunt John built a swimming pool. Now I could just sleep in my swimsuit and fall into the pool. By the way, my swimsuit covered my body, not from head to toe, but in the 1950s, we wore one-piece suits that covered my rear and my cleavage. What an exciting time to be at Aunt John's. However, one day, I had a big problem when we had drained the pool in order to clean it. Oh yeah, we had suds up our brooms and were scrubbing away in the diving well when, all of a sudden, my feet slid out from under me; and I hit the back of my head on the concrete. I was out like a light. They took me to the doctor's office and the doctors determined I had a concussion. I can remember getting a letter, which I kept because it stated that I was normal.

Some of the distressing things I remember during the summers were bats flying down to the pool and drinking water at night. This was the one thing I was fearful of—that they would fly down and get lice in my beautiful long blond hair. How silly, but I was really afraid. Some other things that were not much fun were the chiggers that I would get when we picked blackberries up on the hill, or my allergy to poison ivy. Then I'd get impetigo from scratching the mosquito bites; oh boy, those mosquitoes loved my blood. Since I was a tomboy, I'd get many cuts, scrapes, or scratches while playing, and I can remember Momma or someone asking me, "What happened?" I promise I couldn't remember how in the world I had hurt myself and had a big gash with dried blood on my leg!

Among all the fun activities I would do during my summer visits were the wonderful times I had at the Atlanta Crackers' baseball games. They were so much fun, and of course, we had to have hot dogs, popcorn, peanuts, Cracker Jacks, and Coca-Cola. I can't remember what I enjoyed most, the food or the games. Earl Mann, the owner of the Crackers, was one of my Aunt John's patients. Guess where we had season tickets—box seats right on the first base line.

I could go on forever about our fun times in Norcross; however, some of the best times were at the Swan Theatre in downtown Norcross. Mr. and Mrs. Zebell were the owners and all the kids in Norcross would be at the theater every Saturday for double feature cowboy movies. Some of my favorite cowboys were Hopalong Cassidy, Roy Rogers, Lash LaRue, Gene Autry, and the Lone

Ranger with Tonto. Along with the main features, we would also have a newsreel and cartoons. What an afternoon! Sometimes I would be bad. I liked to catch lightning bugs in mayonnaise jars, take them into the theater, and let them out. They were so bright in that dark place. Bugs Mimm's Rexall drugstore was right next door where we could get a hot fudge sundae at the soda fountain. Life was good.

Since summers in Norcross were so much fun, I wanted to share this experience with my good friend Adrienne. The summer when we were thirteen, Adrienne went with me on the train to Grandmother's. This is one of those true confessions that I'm not sure if I ever told anyone in my life. Well, Adrienne and I were in the club car of the train, and there were these young navy guys. They were so friendly and cute; they offered us a cigarette. Well, we didn't take it because we didn't know how to smoke. We excused ourselves and bought a package of Lucky Strikes and went off to the ladies' room to practice. By the way, back then, there was not a skull and crossbones on the package warning you that cigarettes could kill you. Besides, all my relatives except my grandmother smoked, including my mother and father. So we practiced for a while, then looked for our new cute friends, but they were nowhere to be found. Fortunately, Adrienne and I did not get addicted to cigarettes, and that was the end of my smoking.

After we arrived in Atlanta, we did all the regular events. I really had a great time sharing my special farm with my best friend. I must add that Dodger especially enjoyed Adrienne's visit as well. Remember that all the boys loved having Adrienne around, and Dodger, like so many others, had a crush on her.

CHAPTER FIVE

WE GET OUR OWN HOUSE

When our lease was up at the Haynes house, Daddy and Momma finally decided to buy our own house, so we moved to E. William David Parkway. It was a three-bedroom house with one bath and no air-conditioning; however, we did have an attic fan that tried to keep us cool during the hot, sultry New Orleans summers. We had a floor heater that kept our house warm in the winters. Our house was very nice, but not as large as the Haynes house, which was only about two miles away. Fortunately, it kept me in the same school district; however, as I mentioned, our eighth grade was sent down to Metairie Grammar School. This was to be my last year in school with Adrienne. There were many changes occurring during this year. Looking back on it now, I see it as a time of becoming more responsible and discovering myself. Boys became a bigger issue, and I can remember Mr. Maitre taking us to the eighth grade prom in that lovely Cadillac. I did look feminine in my lovely formal gown.

However, like so many times of maturing, all was not enjoyable during my time at Metairie Grammar. Two unpleasant incidents come to mind. The first occurred when I copied someone's homework in my English class and my teacher, Mrs. Lacy, caught me. She asked me to stay after class and was really hurt that I had done this. She was so nice; I apologized and promised not to do it again. I can't remember if she punished me or not; all I can recall is that I was very embarrassed and ashamed.

The other unpleasant learning experience was Momma's trying to make me well-rounded. You see, she had this special gift of being able to play the piano by ear. If you could hum it, Momma could play it. When I was thirteen years old, Momma decided that I needed to learn to play the piano, so off I went to piano lessons. This was a very humbling experience for me. Here I was, fully grown at five feet, eight inches tall and weighed about 140 pounds. Remember, I was already happily into my sports, and now I was going to take piano lessons. Anyway, I tried and practiced for a few months until it was time for the spring recital. Well, the piece the teacher wanted me to play was called "Climbing." Actually, get this—it was just going up the piano scales. To top it off, you should have seen the little young girls playing *real* music.

Fortunately, Momma didn't make me go back. That was the end of my musical career. In fact, my musical abilities were so bad that years later, when I took a tambourine to my church to worship the Lord, the musicians asked me not to bring it anymore because I really got their beat all mixed up. Let's face it—I was really lacking any musical abilities. I loved to sing in church but needed someone else's strong voice to keep me on key. If we clapped to the music, I had to look at someone else who knew when to clap—I was really bad!

Something else I hate to admit is that I read my first book, *Rookie First Baseman*, in the eighth grade. Yes, I played first base. During the maturing process at Metairie Grammar, there was another activity that I really enjoyed—marbles. Now that I think about it, maybe it didn't have anything to do with my maturing; however, this was a game that we played in the yard during recess and lunch. I was really proud when I could capture some boy's shooter, or we called it something like *bolley*. We played for keeps, and I tried to get all the boys' marbles into my bag. During recess and lunch, we also played dodgeball. There was one girl's game I liked—jacks.

Before Adrienne left me, God put another special friend in my life at Metairie Grammar, and it's funny—she also had a really cool mom named Corky. My new friend was Jackie Villars. They lived above her father's roofing business for a while. Jackie was also athletic. It was fortunate that I met Jackie, since after Adrienne started to attend Newman High School in the ninth grade, we lost touch for many years. Oddly enough, I kept in touch with her mom and visited her when I was in New Orleans for the Republican National Convention in 1988. In 2007, I went again to New Orleans to see the terrible damage that Hurricane Katrina had done to my hometown. Then Mrs. Maitre was in a charming assisted living home. She still had that sparkle in her dark brown eyes, and we had a wonderful time reminiscing the days gone by. However, I had to speak very loudly; her ears were her only problem. For someone born in 1911, she was still an amazing lady, and I'm glad God put her in my mother's life and mine.

While riding my bike to Metairie Grammar School that year, I would stop on the way home to watch the kids playing volleyball at a catholic school. The nuns finally asked me to join them, and I had many enjoyable afternoons playing volleyball there. This was a new sport that I really grew to love, especially the part of slamming the ball down on the girls on the other side of the net. We graduated from eighth grade, and the next year I got to go back to Metairie High School for my freshman year.

As far as school was concerned, I was a good student, but not a brain like Alfred Hew, who was two years older, and his sister, Pat, who was in my grade. They were Asians and really applied themselves, especially Alfred, who was valedictorian of his class. Maybe I could have been an even better student if my sports had not gotten in the way, because when I started high school, it was as if someone said, "Let the games begin!" I would play volleyball in the fall, basketball in the winter, softball in the spring, bowling all year round, and spend lots of time swimming in the summer. I was elected vice president of my freshman class and was also on the student council. My freshman class voted me the Most Active and Best Athlete. I enjoyed school and can remember taking a mechanical drawing class; I was the only girl with nineteen boys. Our teacher was Mr. R. J. Prinz. No no, it was not the boys; I really had considered going to Georgia Tech and studying architecture. However, would you believe they would not let girls go to their university back then?

Loved my basketball at Metairie High School (1954)

You might say I was boy-crazy, or at least my mother thought I was. I really did like a boy from Norcross named Hilton Johnson. (I'd gotten over Tommy by now!) He was really cute, with blue eyes and black hair, dressed in his blue jeans with a white dress shirt. We called his look "frat," and then there were others that we called "cats" because they were greasy-looking with ducktails (their long hair was swept up from their faces like duck tails!). Obviously, I liked the frats! Hilton was very athletic with a sweet personality. I got along really well with his mom, PK (for Pearl Katie). We only got to see each other during the summer and at Christmas. However, in my sophomore year, I had my cartilage taken out of my left knee and lived with Aunt John from October 17, 1953, until after Christmas.

I attended Sacred Heart High School for part of my sophomore year while I was rehabilitating from my surgery. Unbelievable now, but they hospitalized me for seven days with a cartilage! By then, my muscles had all atrophied, so I had to go to rehabilitation for weeks to build them back up. Therefore, during this long period, I went to Sacred Heart because it was on the same campus as Marist, the boys' school that my cousins, Danny and Dodger, attended along with Hilton and Tommy. This was the first of many surgeries; in fact, the latest count is seven on my knees, which were replaced on February 19, 1996. My hips have both been replaced as well—the right one in 2000 and the left one in 2006. I have always bragged about the fact that after my last hip was replaced on Tuesday, I walked a mile on Saturday with one crutch! Hips are easy.

Even though I spent the time in Atlanta that year, I still got to play enough sports at Metairie to be chosen Most Athletic. I was the girls' sports editor and wrote for the school newspaper, the *Jacket's Buzz*. We had a bowling league, and I was vice president. After I got back from my knee operation, I was able to play some basketball, and we went to the state tournament. This was a special time for me, even though I played horribly and got so frustrated when this little guard would not even let me get out of my corner. It was special because Daddy took off from work to drive us up to Lafayette, Louisiana, for the tournament.

I also need to mention my coach, Miss Mary McEniry, who always made me feel so special. Miss Mac even let me practice with the varsity softball team when I was in seventh grade. She was my coach for all the different sports, and I really enjoyed playing for her. I have kept in touch with her and visited her in Gulfport, Mississippi, in 2007. Bob and I took her to dinner. This was after we had visited New Orleans and saw Mrs. Maitre and then Tu-Tu. I will always call her Miss Mac even though she married Ed Wedding after I left New Orleans. When we visited her, I was so blessed to see that she was still so spry in her eighties.

Hilton and I dated for about a year until I really messed up our relationship. While I was at Sacred Heart, we had a Sadie Hawkins dance—you know, where the girls get to invite the boys. I asked Hilton, but he didn't want to go. Well, headstrong me wanted to go. I thought, *I'll show him*, and I did. I invited Tom "Toehead" Skinner to take me, and he accepted. Uh-oh—bad move. Hilton came to the dance but just sat there all night and watched me. That was the end of our relationship. I didn't realize how much I had hurt him until I went to his house the next day, and his mother, PK, told me that not only did I hurt him, but he was over at Nancy Garner's house. I knew that this was the girl who had liked him for a long time, and actually, they ended up getting married.

After Hilton and I broke up, I was devastated, but then along came a handsome football player that went to Metairie. I remember there was a song back in the mid-1950s, "Puppy Love." Anyway, this was not just puppy love. "His name was Andrew Anthony "Frenchie" Trosclair; we had our first date on April 23, 1954. We went steady for almost three years. He was a Cajun and could speak French. One time, I went with him and his family to Bayou Lafourche to visit his grandmother, and they only spoke French. I had never been down in Cajun country before, and it was a very different environment. Her house was built out over the bayou on stilts and was very rustic. We were sitting around in a circle, and I knew when they were talking about me because they would all look my way and smile! I'm glad we didn't stay but a couple of hours because I couldn't join in on the conversation, and I do like to converse. There's another confession that I wish I didn't have to write about. Even though I didn't lose my virginity with Frenchie, I am ashamed of the hot and heavy making out we did. Now it seems this is not that important to the young people today, but most of my friends and I valued waiting until we got married to go all the way. I am also grateful that he never took advantage of my vulnerability. I was in love with Frenchie, and he was in love with me. Life was good.

I say life was good, but then I remember a real problem that we, as young people, faced in the 1950s—*polio*. This disease came really close to my life at Metairie High School. There was another cheerleader with me, Carolyn Fittere, who got it. She was a very pretty brunette with lovely dark brown eyes and was very popular. We had been warned that we could get this disease in Lake Pontchartrain; actually, they didn't know where we all could get it, especially in the summertime. This was before Jonas Salk developed the vaccine to prevent this dreaded disease on April 12, 1955. I can still remember Carolyn coming to the football game in an ambulance with her iron lung on her. Carolyn was the co-queen for our homecoming game in 1954.

Another thing I can remember about this football season was how I liked to show off on the sidelines; in between my cheerleading, I'd be passing the football. I could really throw it far—not like a girl, but like a guy. Well, it really pleased me that Coach Schexnaidre noticed and told me that he wanted me to come out and give his quarterback a lesson. I never knew if he was teasing or not, but I have always told the story as though he was not teasing!

Loved being a Metairie High School cheerleader (1954)

Something that I really enjoyed about living in New Orleans was the great food, especially the great Italian food at Pete Sclafani's. Also, Wellswood Restaurant, out over the Huey P. Long Bridge on Highway 90, had great steaks and Italian bread. The hot roast beef po'boys were wonderful all around New Orleans, especially at Mother's down by the Mississippi River, off Canal Street. I know it's about sixty years ago, and I can still remember. Remember, I have this food problem—I love it!

Our crabbing times out at Lake Pontchartrain were really fun. We'd take our chicken or beef bones and put them in the flat baskets, then throw them into the lake until we could see the crabs come for a bite. We'd pull them up real fast and throw them in our large box. We'd take them home and watch the blue crabs turn red as we boiled them live. Sometimes we would go to the lakefront and eat crabs, usually on a Friday night. We liked to sit out over the water in a very rustic restaurant where we could eat those crabs, using a knife to open the claws. It was fun as the juice from the crabs rolled down our arms—really messy. Oh! Momma also liked the yellow eggs and fats that were in the females. That always grossed me out! So I liked to eat the male crabs and it was easy to tell the difference—their little marking on the bottom of their shell was skinny, and the female's was wide. However, these hard-shelled crabs didn't fill you up, and we always had a fried fish sandwich after the crabs.

A real eye-opener was when we would park and then walk to the restaurant; we'd have to go past Club My-O-My. This club had the most fascinating pictures in front. Would you believe there were men impersonating women and they were gorgeous. Daddy told me that one time he was fooled into buying one of them a drink thinking the guy was a sexy girl!

CHAPTER SIX

WE MOVE TO ATLANTA

Here I was in the middle of my junior year at Metairie—remember, life was good. I was on the volleyball, basketball, and softball teams; president of the varsity club; on the school newspaper staff; on the student council; and a cheerleader. Also, I don't know how it happened because I moved to Atlanta in January of 1955, but I was elected Most Popular, Most Active, and Best Athlete. What a match—the love of my life, Frenchie, was elected Handsomest, Best Athlete, and Most Active. I had mixed emotions when Daddy told me that we would be moving to Atlanta. Of course, I loved Atlanta and had already had a taste of going to school at Sacred Heart, but just to think of leaving Frenchie, my good friend Jackie, and all my other friends was really hard. Fortunately, the decision was not mine to make, so on that cold winter day in January, my friends and teammates came to the airport and watched as I got on the plane headed for Atlanta.

I started the next week at Sacred Heart. I really liked the school; however, it was a lot smaller than Metairie. Something that helped me accept the change was that I knew Metairie was going to become

East Jefferson Consolidated High School. In our senior year, our class was to be merged with other rival high schools in the area.

Fortunately, I got to Sacred Heart in time to play on the basketball team. This helped me adjust to the change, along with having my cousins, Danny and Dodger, right next door at Marist. Another thing that was special was the 1951 sea foam green Ford convertible that Momma and Daddy bought me. They bought a really lovely home in Brookhaven on Ashford Dunwoody Road, close to Oglethorpe University. It was very nice, right across from a private golf course, with a big yard that my daddy got to mow. Don't ask me why, but I can remember getting two snakes while I lived there. One was a king snake and the other was a copperhead. I must have been crazy! I was not afraid of snakes, remember—just bats. Momma wouldn't let me keep them at home, so I had to keep them down by a lake close to our house.

Wow! Was I surprised that some of the girls at this Catholic high school actually went into the bathrooms and smoked cigarettes. However, God provided me with two really good girlfriends, Carolyn Schaeffer and Gail Rogers. In fact, we still get together every August for our birthday celebration. Gail ended up being married to my cousin Scooter for a brief time. As a side note, Scooter ended up married to my good friend Sylvia Cape (Tommy's sister) for many years. Anyway, Carolyn lived in Chamblee, really close to our house, and we spent lots of time together. I can remember our having a birthday party for our dogs! I took Tiny Two over to visit with Carolyn's dog, Queenie. What fun, their toenails looked so lovely after the manicure we gave them! I don't know if they enjoyed it half as much as Carolyn and I did. Life was good.

One bad thing about going to Sacred Heart was the fact that we lived a long way from downtown Atlanta, where the school was located. I took the bus from Oglethorpe, which was the end of the line to go all the way into Atlanta; it took over an hour. I got to wear a uniform at Sacred Heart and this saved me a lot of time. It was a navy skirt and navy vest with a white blouse. To stay warm, we could wear a navy sweater. The outfit was complete with our navy and white saddle oxfords—we really looked good.

My class had only about thirty-three girls in it. I really loved my principal, Sister Kathleen Marie. Behind her back, I called her Sister Katie Mae. The nuns really taught us to respect authority, so whenever an adult came into our class, we would have to stand until they told us to sit.

I was doing fine and had even gotten over Frenchie to some extent. There was this boy next door named Tom Stull, who I had started dating. I didn't tell Frenchie about Tom, and would you believe, the next thing I knew, Frenchie was coming to Atlanta for a visit that summer. It was a little awkward at first. Frenchie stayed with my cousin Dodger. It seems so strange now, but he ended up moving to Norcross and attended Marist with Dodger and Danny for his senior year. Frenchie and I were back together.

So my life was complete, except no volleyball, softball, or bowling; Sacred Heart only played basketball. In my senior year, I was once again a cheerleader, co-captain of the basketball team, and president of my senior class. Getting to be president of the class was kind of tricky because I remember there was some confusion between the grade transcripts of Metairie and Sacred Heart. You had to have a B average to be a class officer. I was not on the list! I knew that I would be elected president if I was, so I jumped up and ran down three flights of stairs to explain to Sister Kathleen Marie that I did have that average and finally she agreed. Then I raced back up the stairs, and I was elected president.

I did well in my senior year scholastically, except I lost the GPA that I needed to remain in the beta club because of a C in Spanish. I certainly enjoyed the basketball and was co-captain of the team. Because of this, Sister Kathleen Marie thought I would do just fine to play in the Atlanta High School Tennis Tournament! Hey, wait a minute, Sister! I had never played tennis. But Mary Kay Judy, the captain, knew how to play; so she and I went to the tournament to represent Sacred Heart. Mary Kay actually won a match. I didn't.

In the spring of 1956, I suffered another problem with my knees. I had been told that when I had the left one operated on in my sophomore year, the cartilage in my right knee was cracked; and when it broke, it would be a lot worse than my left one. They were right. I went back to Saint Joseph's for another long stay in the hospital—nine days—and they removed the broken piece of cartilage from my right knee. And again there was a long rehab time.

Frenchie and I continued our romance, and I was his senior sponsor for Marist. It wasn't any big honor; I just accompanied him at a parade around the campus and got my picture in the *Marist Annual*.

Frenchie and me (1956)

Right before graduation, my teachers at Sacred Heart gave me an award that I have always cherished. I believe I have even appreciated it more because I wasn't even a Catholic. The award that I received was the Atlanta Journal Cup for Best All-Around Student. How it has blessed me to have polished that silver cup all these years. Our graduation took place in Sacred Heart Catholic Church on May 25, 1956.

My senior picture for the *Annual*

Finally, I was out of high school and headed to college. Shockingly, one of my classmates, shortly after graduation, was headed to the hospital to deliver a baby! No one had suspected this scandal. Remember, along with our uniforms, we could wear a navy sweater, and that is exactly what Joann did—a very full sweater. Well, anyway, I was headed to Louisiana State University—home of the LSU Tigers—while Joann was home taking care of her little one. Frenchie also applied to LSU, and our college careers began that fall semester, 1956. Life was good.

Chapter Seven

College Days

G oing to college was a really big deal for me. It had been a lifelong goal. Mother and Daddy drove me to LSU, where I shared a room with two other girls. We shared a small bathroom with our suitemates who had a room on the other side. A larger bathroom was down the hall and all the girls on our floor shared it. I was in the freshman dorm called Evangeline Hall. My roommates were Joan Burns and Beverly "something." They were really nice, and we loved each other immediately, so now I knew someone else on campus besides Frenchie. Momma helped me get my bed and little area of the room decorated. It was an old dorm with very high ceilings. This dorm was probably built shortly after they started admitting girls in 1906. Yes, this was the fiftieth anniversary remembering when seventeen brave young girls came to LSU. Then Momma and Daddy left me. The cafeteria was located next to our dorm, so I knew I wasn't going to starve to death.

I really established a close relationship with Joan and Beverly; they called me Mommacita. They probably gave me this term of endearment because I was selected to be the floor monitor for all the girls on our floor, and I had to take care of them, as in saying, "Shh" when lights were out at 9:00 PM. Another thing that I remember was watching one of the really popular girls vomiting in the communal bathroom. This really sent me a strong message, and although Momma and Daddy had been drinking alcohol throughout my life, I probably never had more than ten drinks in my whole life. It just seemed stupid to spend your money and be out of control; besides, Coca-Cola tasted better anyway. Alcoholism ran in my family, and I realized that if I didn't drink alcohol, I would not have this problem.

I enrolled as a business administration major. Classes were okay, and I passed everything. I had always been an LSU football fan, so I enjoyed going to the games at Tiger Stadium which really rocked on a Saturday night. Sorry to say, we lost every game. Have no fear, we had a player in my freshman class, Billy Cannon, who was to turn all those losses into wins for the next three years as he became an All-American.

It's funny but sad how a lot of kids stop going to church when they go off to college or are on their own. However, from the time I was saved in Metairie, I attended church regularly. After we moved to Atlanta, I attended Brookhaven First Methodist Church by myself. So it didn't take me long to find a church in Baton Rouge. There were two other events that stand out in my college days at LSU. One occurred in November 1956. I got to vote for the first time in my young life. How special it was for me, because Georgia was the only state in the forty-eight that allowed eighteen-year-olds to vote, and fortunately, I had just turned eighteen in August. Therefore, I got an absentee ballot and voted at the post office in Baton Rouge. I had been campaigning for Dwight D. Eisenhower since he announced his candidacy on March 12, 1952. His slogan for both campaigns was "I like Ike," and that I did. I was so fortunate to get to vote for his second term as president.

The other event was so exciting as well; we had a panty raid at Evangeline Hall. I can still see the hundreds of boys coming across the dark field toward our dorm. They had torches and were shouting, "Throw us your panties! We want your panties!" We were told to turn out the lights and keep the windows shut. Since I was the floor monitor, I had to make sure the girls followed the instructions. But alas, some of the girls not only opened their windows, but they also threw some panties down to the crazy guys. We had guys climbing up on the side of the dorm, shouting for more panties. Fortunately, the police came and got things under control; no one was hurt. What a night to remember!

I didn't stay at LSU very long. At Christmastime, I went home and met Frank Reeves, the captain of Alabama Polytechnic Institute's football team. I met him at Aunt John's, and we began dating. So I told Daddy that I wanted to transfer to API in Auburn, Alabama. Auburn was a lot closer to Atlanta, so Daddy said yes. LSU was on the semester system, and I had to go back after Christmas to complete my classes. I can still remember telling Frenchie goodbye and giving him his class ring, sweater, and ID bracelet back. I kissed him goodbye on the front stairs of Evangeline Hall. It still makes me sad, even now; he was a good guy, and I was a jerk.

Unfortunately, Auburn was on the quarter system, and I had to wait for the quarter to begin. I had worked for Southern Bell

Telephone and Telegraph Company the summer before, right after I graduated from high school. They placed me in the cost accounting department and my supervisor was Martha Slaton. I hate to tell you, but I'm sure I lied and told them I was not going to college when they hired me. However, Martha wanted me back during the break between schools.

I started to attend Auburn in March 1957, and I lived in Dorm IX. I only had one roommate on the third floor, though I really can't remember her at all. I did make a good friend down the hall from me, Jerry Williamson. Jerry was from Birmingham, Alabama. At Auburn, I changed my major to physical education with a math minor. I am really glad I did because I could take a tennis class and a combination senior lifesaving/water safety instructor class. Many years later, I was so grateful for the calculus class that I also took and made a B. Well, needless to say, Frank and I did not last too long. He was getting ready to graduate, and I was just too immature for him. Besides, he drank a lot.

CHAPTER EIGHT

THE LIFE CHANGER

I really liked Auburn and was planning on going back for the fall quarter. However, a lot happened during summer break. I had dated some after Frank, but no one in particular. That summer, I applied to the City of Atlanta for a lifeguard job and got hired. I was assigned to Garden Hills Pool in Buckhead. It was a small pool in an old established neighborhood, and I guarded as well as taught swimming. Then they transferred me to the gigantic pool at Chastain Park located in North Fulton. Since the pool was much larger, there were several other lifeguards on duty with me. I was the first girl lifeguard in Atlanta. I guess the only reason that I have always said this through the years was because I was on a WSB television program called *Today in Georgia*, and when Ruth Kent interviewed me, that was her primary focus.

Lifeguard Charlotte on duty

Since I was a girl, I didn't have to hose down the deck and do all of those awful cleanup jobs. It was fun, and I started dating one of the other guards, George W., who was a senior at Georgia Tech. When it rained, we would play cards in the pump house and get paid while we goofed off! Remember how I told you that I believed when people teased me it was because they really liked me? Well, many of the kids called me Moby Dick; I'm positive it was because they liked me and the fact that I wore a white swimsuit. I was sure I looked good because I had gotten a great tan from all the baby oil with iodine that I poured on my skin. Toward the end of the summer, I met someone who would change my life forever—Bob Czekala.

Bob, the handsome paratrooper that stole my heart

In August of 1957, I noticed these good-looking guys swimming at Chastain Park Pool. You couldn't miss them because they didn't swim much but were walking around the big pool on their hands. Well, actually, one of them had these great big bulging muscles and could walk all the way around the very large fifty-meter pool. One of the other ones had a nice build, but couldn't walk all the way around the pool. That's the one I liked, Bob Czekala. What a weird name; I not only learned to pronounce it but also managed to spell it—very quickly! We all got to talking, and I found out that they were in the army's honor guard company who were stationed at Fort McPherson. Bob was a paratrooper and had done many jumps. They were only in Atlanta for a few weeks to perform at the Chastain Park Amphitheater, which was right up the hill from the pool. I went to one of their performances and did they ever look sharp in their uniforms, doing all the precision drill tricks they had been taught. After several days, we got acquainted, and they wanted to know of any clubs around Atlanta where we could go. So the big party girl, who I wasn't, said, "Sure." I had heard of one in downtown Atlanta, close to the Fox Theatre right off Ponce de Leon Avenue. I can't recall the name, but I do remember that it was a really wild strip club! Well, don't be alarmed; after growing up in New Orleans, I had been to a strip club at the tender age of thirteen with my boyfriend, O. G. Martin. It wasn't that big a deal; I had gone with OG and his parents, with my parents' permission, to see the beautiful Oyster Girl, all curled up nude on a big oyster shell. Anyway, back to our outing in Atlanta. We went, and everyone had a good time. That night, when I told the guys good night, Bob kissed me while I was sitting in my car and he was standing outside. We had planned on a date the next morning—to go to Mass at Sacred Heart Church. What a paradox, strip club to church.

Well, the way Bob tells it, I came squealing into the church parking lot on two wheels in my daddy's big Buick as he stood waiting for me in front of the church. I can't dispute this because I did drive too fast, and I was always in a hurry to be on time, which was almost impossible for me to accomplish. That's a nice way of saying that I was usually late. From the very beginning, our relationship blossomed rapidly. Bob's time in Atlanta ended right after my nineteenth birthday. In August, he went back to his home base in Fort Campbell, Kentucky. This long distance did not deter the progression of our romance. We wrote love letters and talked occasionally on the phone, which was very expensive. I learned that he was or had been engaged to a girl in Chicago named Janet, but this did not get in my way of pursuing him.

Now my dilemma—what about college? Remember my lifelong goal? Well, I had another lifelong goal as well—to get married when I was nineteen. Don't ask me why! I was smart, but did not have a brain that could graduate college by nineteen. Anyway, I went back to Auburn for the sorority rush week before classes began. I ended up not pledging any. Jerry and I were to be roommates, but I got to thinking that if I stayed in college, Bob will not ask me to marry him. So with this thought, I went back to Atlanta and started working at Southern Bell again. Momma didn't mind at all; she saw no reason for a girl to go to college, and daddy was once again supportive of whatever I wanted to do.

After I went back to Southern Bell, they knew I had been a lifeguard and a water safety instructor, so they asked me to go to the Atlanta YMCA and teach a young girl while they wrote an article about me in their newspaper.

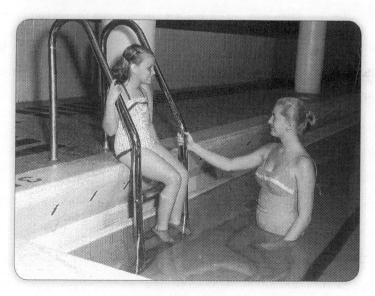

I began early as a swimming instructor (1957)

Here's another historical fact. This one was very significant; the Soviet Union's *Sputnik 1* was successful on October 4, 1957. There was much ado about this. I can remember our local hamburger restaurant had a Sputnik burger on the menu! Here we were in the middle of the Cold War with Russia from after the end of World War II until December 25, 1991, and they had this space contraption. During the Cold War with Russia, on June 12, 1987, the Soviet Union was having a problem in their part of Berlin, Germany, and built a wall to keep their people from defecting to the western part of the city. I loved our president, Ronald Reagan, and during his presidency, he told the Soviet leader, Mikhail Gorbachev, "Tear down this wall!" It took a couple of years, but during George H. W. Bush's presidency on November 9, 1989, the wall came tumbling down. The people of West Berlin were once again able to visit loved ones, work, and even move to the more lucrative American-administered side of Berlin. At this point in history, the world found out that the Russians were not the superpower that people thought they were. This country that was thought to be so strong had major problems; it began to crumble. During this "war," neither Bob nor our troops were ever involved in any combat.

I was right about coming home from school if I wanted to get married. Bob would drive to Atlanta in his old car until he totaled it. That didn't stop him from being with me! He started hitchhiking down and back on the weekends. In a very short time, we were planning on getting married. Well, Bob was twenty-three, and things got pretty hot and heavy; the bottom line is I lost my virginity in the front seat of his car. I know that this was not God's best for me, and I have always regretted this sin. I really never expected this to happen. How could I? As a Christian, I was really sorry and believed, at the time, that in God's eyes, we were married after becoming "one flesh." I have since changed my mind, not about staying a virgin until the vows are made, but the part about having to get married because you had sex. There was never an actual date that we got engaged—probably right before Christmas. It's hard to say exactly because I didn't want an engagement ring. I guess it sounds strange that I didn't want an engagement ring, but I had big hands and knew he couldn't afford a diamond large enough. So I just wanted a wide gold wedding band. Our favorite song at the time was "Chances Are," sung by Johnny Mathis—so romantic.

After Christmas, I went to Chicago to meet Bob's parents, my future in-laws. I was in for a big shock. This was my first time in the North. One day, while I was there, I was on a bus trying to decide whether it was my stop or not. Then this lady waiting to get on the bus said, "Damn it, either get off or move out of the way." Where was the Southern charm that I was used to? However, this was not the most upsetting aspect of my visit. Bob's family was a mess. I had never been in this type of environment. They lived in a small dingy apartment. Bob had always slept in the kitchen and had grown up in a completely different lifestyle than mine.

His mother, Florence, was very nice and had worked as a waitress for many years. She had been married to three alcoholic husbands. (After we married, she married two more!) At least I think she had married all of them. Bob was very confused about what last name he had used when different alcoholic men entered his life at various times. He never knew his biological father, Edwin Czekala, who left Flo before Bob was two. Then a man named Ellett came into Bob's life before he entered school. Bob used his name until he was drafted as Robert Czekala in 1956. Ellett only stayed a couple years, and then Bob had a new "father" named McPherson. Mac was part of Bob's life until he died several years after we were married. He had been a chef from New York and was working at the racetrack in Chicago. I'm not sure how bad the alcoholism was in the first two fathers, but Mac had a serious problem. He was drunk and disheveled all the time. Later, Bob would tell me of his horrendous childhood that included beatings, attempted drownings in the bathtub, and many other atrocities.

During this visit, we went ice-skating outdoors in fifteen-below-zero weather. Yes, this little Southern girl learned to ice-skate in order to impress my boyfriend! I did not like the cold.

Bob had lived in this environment until he went into the military at twenty-one. Life was not good. You know they say love is blind, and in my mind I was already married to this man, so let's get on with it. I went back to Atlanta, and we continued with our marriage plans. Bob had signed up after the Korean War (1950-1953) and served for two years as a paratrooper. He got discharged on February 19, 1958, when he went back to Chicago to make money. Fortunately, he had been a journeyman printer at Sherwin-Williams before he volunteered to be drafted by the army. We set our wedding date for July 5, 1958. Daddy was not too happy about this.

He said, "You don't even know him. Why don't you marry Frenchie? At least you know him!"

I don't remember Momma being as vocal.

I remember telling Daddy, "All my life, you've allowed me to be responsible and make my own decisions. Now you're telling me what to do!"

He said, "Yes, but this is the most important decision you will ever make."

He said all this without even knowing much about my experience in Chicago at Christmas.

CHAPTER NINE

TWO BECOME ONE

We went on with our wedding plans. One thing that changed was our intimacy ended. Of course, I was sorry it had ever happened and told Bob that our wedding night was not going to be anything special if we continued to have sex.

Something that Bob and I had to consider was his religion. The fact that Bob was Catholic upset Momma and Daddy. They told me they were not happy about my becoming a Catholic. Momma had been raised by a strong Baptist mother who was very prejudiced against Catholics. Daddy was just as upset but was adamant that we would not live in Chicago. PTL! We figured that Bob was accustomed to the South and that I would be happier here. Converting to Catholicism didn't bother me at all. Remember, I had been raised in New Orleans where "everyone" was a Catholic; then I graduated from a Catholic high school. I had loved the nuns and even my best friend, Carolyn, was a Catholic. No big deal. I also believed that, according to the Catholic Church's teaching, Bob would think he was going to hell if he married outside the Catholic Church. So I took classes with Father John Stapleton at Our Lady of Assumption Catholic Church, located right behind our house in Chamblee. I had been sprinkled when I was saved in the Methodist Church, but I needed to be baptized by pouring in the Catholic Church. Father Stapleton baptized me; Carolyn's mother, Ruth Schaeffer, was my sponsor.

So let's see—our plans were finalized; I found a brand new apartment. I could even walk from 834 Argonne Avenue to work at Fourth and Peachtree. This was good, since we only had one car. We selected July 5 so we would have the day off before the wedding. The wedding would be at Sacred Heart, and Father Stapleton would perform the ceremony. I bought my dress off the rack at a store about two blocks from work called Franklin Simons. Carolyn was to be my maid of honor, and Bob's best man was his longtime friend Harlow Lusk. Our reception was to be at Aunt John's pool house in Norcross, and we would go to Panama City Beach for our honeymoon, which was partly funded by Harlow.

Momma and Daddy had the rehearsal dinner at their house. Bob, his mother, and Harlow arrived the day before the rehearsal dinner. I noticed that Bob's hair was really long; he had a shaggy crew cut that desperately needed a haircut. He did go the morning of the wedding—and got scalped! It was not a big wedding. I made my veil out of an old white hat to which I attached nylon tulle. We kept it simple and the service ended with our taking Communion together. I was really glad that we got married at Sacred Heart where I had graduated high school. It was and still is a beautiful old church with stained glass windows and many beautiful paintings and sculptures. It was built at the end of the nineteenth century and is located at 353 Peachtree Street. The reception that Aunt John provided was very nice. She always did a wonderful job with anything. After the reception, we headed for our Florida honeymoon.

L-R: Frank Roper, Carolyn Schaeffer (later married Frank Galvin), Bob, me, Harlow Lusk, and Dodger

Bob and me with Bob's mom—Florence O'Halloran, Daddy, and Momma

Our first night was at a small motel close to Dothan, Alabama. I was very nervous about our first night and did something very out of character for me. I got a bottle of gin from Daddy's stash and had several drinks. I wanted this time to be special for Bob! The next morning, we went to church and spent the next three nights right on the Gulf of Mexico at the Beachcomber Motel. Daddy had taken our family to this beach for many vacations. Bob had never been to a beachfront before, and it was funny that when his legs were peeling from sunburn, he thought the fish were eating his skin. Even with Harlow's financial help, we couldn't stay but a few days; we needed to get home to our one-bedroom apartment.

After our honeymoon, I had to get back to my job. Somebody had to pay the $97.50 rent and buy food. Bob had quit his printing job in Chicago, of course, and he was waiting for the printing union to find him a job in Atlanta. Bob was never lazy and was always willing to do whatever he could. He was waiting for a printing job, but meanwhile, he sold used clothes, worked for a small business making dinette tables, and also sold vacuum cleaners. Bob did not seem like the salesman type, but we laughed when he sold a vacuum to a family that had dirt floors! He actually felt guilty and went back the next day and gave them their money back. Good guy!

Now what does a wife do! When we got married, I really didn't know much about cooking. I can remember cooking corn that had been in the refrigerator for too long and you could not even bite it. I could cook steak, hamburgers, bacon, and eggs. I had received the two volumes of Meta Given's *Modern Encyclopedia of Cooking* as a wedding present. Well, I could read and figured I just had to follow the directions; I did pretty well with this new chore. I hate to admit, but I was really spoiled growing up and never even made my bed until I went to LSU, much less clean and cook. Welcome to the real world!

Our lives were pretty simple during this time. The Krispy Kreme doughnut shop was close by, and we went there often. On Sundays, we would sleep late and after 12:30 PM Mass, we would go out to Chamblee and spend the afternoon with Momma and Daddy. Momma was so good. I would bring our dirty clothes, and she would wash and dry them while Bob, Daddy, and I played a card game called hearts with my Uncle Roddy. We would play for 25¢ a game, while Momma cooked one of her wonderful meals. I believe I really began to appreciate Momma a lot more after I got married.

During the week, we would go bowling or to a movie. I played softball for Southern Bell in a ladies league. In fact, I was asked to play semipro softball with the Atlanta Tomboys for the 1959 season. I had to decline due to some extenuating circumstances. Surprise surprise!

CHAPTER TEN

THE TWO THAT BECAME ONE BECOME THREE

Since we were Catholics and the church didn't approve of birth control, we practiced the rhythm method. I declare this does not work. By September, I had gotten the name of a doctor, William R. Thompson, from a friend at work; I didn't want anyone in the family to know what I was thinking! Yes, lo and behold, I was pregnant. Now you know what we had been doing besides working, playing cards, cooking, cleaning, playing sports, and going to church. Yes, they told me to expect a baby on May 5, 1959. Oh my goodness, as Prissy said in *Gone with the Wind*, "I don't know nothin' 'bout birthin' babies." What in the world were we going to do? Southern Bell required you to go on maternity leave at seven months and Bob was selling vacuum cleaners! As it turned out, God provided. Bob's job came through and he started working for Stein Printing Company before I had to go on leave.

While I worked at Southern Bell, I came up with this new way of billing American Telephone and Telegraph Company for charges that were using Southern Bell lines. This was a big deal for me because I ended up winning a $75 award in 1961. In the 1960s, this was big money, considering I made $45 a week. But anyway, the way I did the billing was to use the computer. Now before I tell you how big the computer was, I want you to know that I was not in the computer department nor was I a keypunch operator. However, I figured out how to use the huge computer that needed to have these cards punched with holes in them in order for the computer to be able to read the information. Well, the computer was the size of a large room! In 1946, when the computer was first used, it needed a thirty-by-sixty-foot room and cost $486,000. I don't believe that our computer was this big, but it was a very large room. Another interesting comparison is that now, in 2009, you can store more information in a microchip about the size of a grain of sand—can you imagine?

I was a proud employee with $75 award!

Well, I had a great pregnancy. I continued to play softball, but now you can see why I had to decline the semipro offer for the next year; I was going to be busy. We bowled in a league. Bob was also a good bowler. After I bowled a 600 series, my enthusiasm waned, and I quit bowling in leagues after that season. I had been bowling since I was six. It was as if I had accomplished a goal, and I have always been a goal-oriented person.

With all of this activity, I was never sick a day until the day Ken was born. On that day, I was really sick; in fact, I was sick as a dog. I thought I had the flu. Well, Momma was worried about me and when Bob left to work his night shift at Stein's downtown, she came over to stay with me. After Momma got there, she said, "Charlotte, I believe you are in labor." I said, "Oh no, Momma, I'm still sewing another maternity top because you told me the first baby is always two weeks late!" Well, at about 5:30 PM, Momma said we'd better go to the hospital and make sure the pains I felt were from the flu. I still remember the pains on the way, but a big one stands out in my mind because it occurred just as I was crossing Linden Avenue to go into the front door of Crawford W. Long Memorial Hospital. I had to stop right there in the middle of the street. Aye aye aye, that was painful! After we checked in, it didn't take them very long to examine me. They told me that I was not in labor and could go home. Fortunately, my doctor was coming to the hospital and he would take a look. I believe they didn't think I was in labor because the baby never dropped into the birth canal and my water had not broken. Anyway, when Dr. Thompson took a look at me, he decided I was in labor. They took me to the delivery room and gave me a shot. I don't remember anything until I woke up and there was this seven-pound, two-ounce baby boy in my arms. Michael Kenneth

Czekala had decided to come two weeks early, April 20, 1959, at 11:23 PM. Yes, nine and a half months after we married, we had our first son. Bob was there when I woke up, so all was well.

This was taken on Ken's first birthday—wasn't he precious?

By the way, remember Momma gained forty pounds with me? The doctor and Momma told me not to gain more than twenty pounds, and I didn't, even if I did gain ten in one month. During my pregnancy, I was so swollen from water retention that I couldn't even wear my bedroom slippers. The biggest problem I had was having my hands so swollen that I could not get my wedding band on and worried about what people might think.

Remember how close I was to Daddy? Well, I have to say that Momma really was the one I had to depend on to help me take care of this baby. We actually moved into their bedroom with Ken's baby bed! Momma took care of me and the baby for about three weeks. I did not nurse Ken because, there again, I listened to Momma and she had had a bad experience trying to nurse me. Besides, nobody was nursing at that time. They gave me a shot right after he was born to prevent my producing milk, but I did anyway, so they took a sheet and wrapped it around me to squeeze out any milk I had! Yes, it was uncomfortable, and now I wish I had nursed. One other problem I had was my blood is A-negative and Bob's is O-positive. Ken got Bob's blood. They explained that I could have one more baby without a problem, but after that, there could be problems with the baby because of the Rh factor.

Father Stapleton baptized Ken at Our Lady of the Assumption on May 24, 1959. Carolyn Schaeffer was his godmother and Harlow Lusk, his godfather. Momma and Daddy had a nice little gathering at their house, including Great-Grandmother Edith, to celebrate the baptism. Everyone seemed excited on this occasion, and I believe Momma and Daddy just loved us.

Remember I promised to share some historical facts to help you understand what was happening during certain times of my life? Well, this is another update. When Ken was born, Dwight D. Eisenhower was still president, and Bob Hope, Frank Sinatra, and Doris Day were popular entertainers. Also, we had a new place to shop in Atlanta—Lenox Square. We didn't have to go downtown to Rich's or Davison's; they were in Buckhead! They even said that one day this area would have large buildings, just like downtown Atlanta. Hard to believe at the time, but how true! Shopping malls became the big thing and popped up all over the United States.

It was the middle of May when we got back into our apartment. Our lease was going to be up the end of June, so we started looking for a two-bedroom apartment out toward Momma's. We decided to move into a two-story apartment at 1433 Meeting Road in Chamblee, about four miles from Momma. The apartments were called Caldwell Village and they looked like army barracks. We had cockroaches flying all over the living room when you turned on the lights until we were able to exterminate them. I will never forget that I had this feeling of vulnerability when I was upstairs in our bedroom next to Ken's. I had always felt confident that I could handle whatever came my way, but now I had this baby to protect and wasn't so sure I could if someone tried to break into our apartment. It didn't help that Bob worked nights and I worked days part-time at Southern Bell. Momma took care of Ken whenever we needed her. I've already told you that Bob was never lazy, and during these years, he would work nights and then take care of Ken in the day until he had to go to work. It was not what we had planned, but we adjusted to the new member of our family. We had a dream and worked hard for it. Life was good.

CHAPTER ELEVEN

OUR DREAM COMES TRUE

For some reason, Bob and I really had a desire to get a home of our own. Of course, I always liked the area out toward Norcross; and in 1961, Momma and Daddy moved out by Grandmother's on Norcross-Tucker Road. Bob and I found a half-acre lot, just inside the Gwinnett County line off Buford Highway. It was a new street that had belonged to the Church of God campground. It cost $2,700, and we made a down payment of $460 on March 25, 1959. The remainder was financed by a man that we didn't even know who would be willing to lend us the balance. We paid him $93.34 a month at 7 percent interest until we paid it off.

Bob and I looked for houses we liked and found one close to our old house over on Ashford Dunwoody Road on Bubbling Creek by the Oglethorpe apartments, just off Harts Mill Road. I got the plans and asked my mother's sister Kathryn Crawford, whom I called Aunt Kappy, to see if her stepson, Ellard Crawford, would oversee the construction. We wanted to build, rather than buy, because Daddy had connections in building supplies; and I had the time to organize and schedule the workers. Daddy was working for Georgia-Pacific but had started Georgia Door and Plywood Services in downtown

Norcross as a side business in 1961. Daddy needed Bob to help him, so Bob quit Stein Printing Company on May 16, 1969, and went to work for Georgia Door. It has blessed and provided for us through the years, even in retirement.

We were able to pay off the lot loan and began building our house on April 29, 1961. Ellard helped us build the house with just a $12,500 loan from Tucker Federal Savings and Loan Association; they charged us 6.5 percent interest, and our payments were $106.77 per month for 244 months. We moved into the house on August 30, 1961; I had just turned twenty-three, and Bob was not quite twenty-seven. It was a lovely old 1,200 square foot brick ranch with a half basement. It had three bedrooms, two bathrooms, a porch across the front, and a long narrow screened back porch. This was a very nice first home.

We were truly blessed, unlike the poor citizens across the Atlantic in Germany; this is the same year that the Russians put up the Berlin Wall. We were truly grateful to be living in the wonderful free republic of the United States of America. Bob and I took advantage of God's provision, and can you believe—shortly after being married three years—we had a baby and a beautiful new house. Our new home had a Doraville address although it was in Gwinnett County—139 Johnson Drive. The neighborhood was nice and quiet with a mixture of young and old couples. An added blessing was a swim and tennis club just over the hill at the end of our cul-de-sac. Unfortunately, it was for the Oakcliff subdivision owners, and they wouldn't let us join until 1962, when they needed more members!

Life was good.

Bob and I both loved animals, so we got a female cocker spaniel mix almost immediately and named her Duncie because her head was pointed. This was the beginning of many animals that we have loved and been blessed with through the years.

When we moved into our new house, Bob and I decided it was time to have another baby. Remember, this was the end of August and can you believe we were expecting our new baby to arrive on June 20? Pretty quick conception again! Robert Lane also came early; he arrived at 11:06 AM on June 14, 1962 (Flag Day). Again, no big deal—I wasn't even sick this time! I just had that pain, then a shot; then I woke up with a new eight-pound, three-ounce baby boy. They checked his blood and he was A-negative. We had taken Ken over to Momma's at 6:30 AM. Bob and I drove to Georgia Baptist Hospital, 300 Boulevard NE, where Lane was delivered by Dr. Abraham S. Velkoff. He was a wonderful Jewish doctor that Aunt John had recommended. Back then, mothers stayed in the hospital for four or five days after giving birth, so I was still in the hospital for Father's Day that year on June 17. The next day, Bob and I took our new little son home.

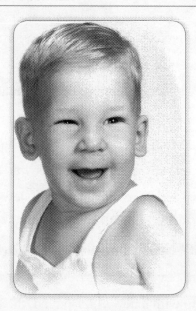

Our precious Lane's first birthday picture

Just for some historical information at this time, Elvis Presley was very popular and so was Bob Hope. John F. Kennedy was our first Catholic president, and the twist was a popular dance.

Lane was dedicated on February 16, 1964. Jo Ann Wells was the godmother and my cousin Dodger was the godfather. The event took place at Northwoods Methodist Church with Reverend Jackson Braddy officiating. I need to explain why Lane was almost two years old for his baptism.

After Ken was born, I knew I didn't want to have a baby every nine months, so Bob agreed, and we started using a contraceptive. Then when we moved to Doraville, there was not a Catholic church in our area, so I started going to Northwoods United Methodist Church. I had also realized by then that Bob had not been brought up in the Catholic Church and was not that devoted to it. He started going with us a few months later, and we joined on February 17, 1963. Our whole family was very active, attending Sunday school and services every Sunday. I was in charge of the church lunches, something I continued doing at every church we'd attend—even our current one. Bob and I were counselors for the Methodist Youth Fellowship for several years and that was a fun time in our life because we would play sports with them and I've always enjoyed being around young people. This reminds me of one Sunday night when we took the youth group to Mount Paran Church of God. Wow, I had not ever been to such a Sprit-filled church—it was wonderful! However, the youth's parents did not appreciate our outing.

We lived a very simple and conservative life. I worked with my Aunt John at Dr. Ralph Murphy's office one night a week helping with the bookkeeping. I later worked part-time in the office at Artsteel. This was a steel fabricator which was close to our house. It was owned by Mr. Claude Brown, who had earned millions in his Brown Transport business. He taught me a lifelong principle. One day, in a meeting, he told us, "You watch the pennies, and I'll watch the millions grow." This now reminds me of a scripture verse—"Those who are faithful in little will be given much."

Later, I kept the books part-time at Brookhaven Supply Company. After we joined the Oaks Country Club, I taught Bob to play tennis. Our whole social life revolved around this club for many years. Of course, we played a lot of tennis. I played with Bob and two other guys, Ron Hill and Joe Ploussard. I taught Ken to swim and he was on the swim team at six. Lane was on the swim team at four. I was very active at the little club and served on the board of directors. Many days, the boys and I would take our lunch down to the pool, and they swam while the moms played bridge. Bob and I played in a couples' bridge club, and I played in a ladies' duplicate club. We did not have any extra money but had all ours needs met. Life was good.

We met a young couple at church, Bill and Liz Crotwell. They were our age and had two girls, Julie and Kim, who were a little younger than our boys. We would go over to their house and play bridge. All the kids had a great time playing. When they got tired, we just put them down on the sofa or somewhere to sleep. Later, after we finished our card game, we picked them up to go home. We had a good time and didn't spend any money; Liz would always have a special dessert, especially her pecan pie! It was rare for us to use babysitters any time, who charged 25 cents an hour! Who could afford that kind of expense! Then the time came when Momma and Daddy decided they just wanted one grandson at a time because Ken and Lane would fight.

I wrote earlier that Momma and Daddy rarely went to church, but God put a young lady in Momma and Daddy's life—Glenda Palmer. Momma worked part-time as a receptionist at Richard Mueller's beauty salon in Buckhead. Glenda worked for him also. She had a real close walk with the Lord, and before I knew it, Momma and Daddy were going to be baptized at Glenda's church. Oh, happy day, my mother and father were baptized at First Baptist Church of Doraville on April 18, 1965. This was a real blessing; Ken and Lane were there with Bob and me. In a little over ten years, both of my parents were to be in heaven with our Heavenly Father.

Our happy family (1965)

Several significant historical events transpired while we lived in this house. The Vietnam War seemed endless, lasting from the mid-1960s until 1975. The country was much divided by this war. In my opinion, we try to help countries all over the world; however, we just don't understand their culture and really don't know what we're doing. I believe that this was the case in Vietnam—there's just no way could we have won. It was difficult to tell the enemy from the allies in all those mountains and jungles. During this war, I can remember a delivery man coming to the front door on November 22, 1963, asking if I had heard that President Kennedy had been assassinated. What a shock! Lee Harvey Oswald was thought to be the lone gunman that killed our president. It was hard to believe that such a thing could happen to our president!

At least one good thing happened during this time; on July 20, 1969, the United States accomplished a great goal! We landed a man on the moon. Yes, Neil Armstrong placed the flag of the USA and said, "That's one small step for man, one giant leap for mankind." Wow, can you believe a man landed on the moon!

As for me and my family, life was good—just swimming, playing tennis, playing bridge, going to functions at church, living close to Momma and Daddy, and taking care of the little guys. Little did I know how much my life would change in the next decade.

CHAPTER TWELVE

THINGS FALL APART—BROKENNESS

As I get to the 1970s, I need to introduce you to my mother's family. Even though I was so much closer with Daddy's people, let's not forget Momma's. I do remember going to see my grandmother, Carrie Strickland Echols, who was born in Milton, Georgia, on November 19, 1875. I vaguely remember that she was frail and had arthritis. Perhaps I remember this from her pictures because she died on April 5, 1943, before I turned five; I really didn't get to know her. I do have a picture of her in her wheelchair and have often wondered if I got her knees because when I was about fifty, I also was in a wheelchair at times. I have a hard time remembering Momma's father, Perry Walter Echols, who was born in Forsyth County, Georgia on January 29, 1876. Even though he lived until I was eight, he spent much of his time in Miami, Florida, with my mother's sister, Kathryn Crawford—my Aunt Kappy.

Perry and Carrie Echols (circa 1941)

However, the family that I got to know best on Momma's side when I was a teenager was her older sister, Placie Marie Barnett (born November 10, 1898), and her family. I don't know how to begin. She was married to Roy T. Barnett (born September 21, 1902); they had a daughter, Carolyn (born January 2, 1929), and a mongoloid son, Ross Thomas "Tommy" (born January 29, 1945). After we moved to Atlanta, occasionally, Momma and Daddy would send me over to stay with them when they went on a trip.

This family's tragedies were the beginning of many sad times for me during the 1970s, when things really started falling apart. This story is very sad. Roy, Marie's husband, was an alcoholic who went on binges sporadically. Aunt Marie was the eldest of the five Echols children. Her daughter, Carolyn, was a very talented pianist and violinist. Carolyn was nine years old when I was born. When I went over to stay with them, I noticed that Roy would come home and Marie would have his dinner on the stove. He would eat alone and then go to his room. No interaction with the family whatsoever. I learned that this was because of his having an affair years before, and Aunt Marie never forgave him. She stopped having all relations with him. However, it doesn't end there; while he was drunk, he raped Marie when she was forty-six, and that's when Tommy was conceived.

Marie was forty-seven when Tommy, a severely handicapped young man, was born, and Marie dedicated the rest of her life to raising Tommy. After I was married, Marie got cancer and died on November 26, 1972. Tommy was twenty-seven. Neither Carolyn nor Roy believed they could take care of Tommy, so they desperately tried to find a good place for him to stay before Marie died. Carolyn was not happy with the results, but felt like she had no choice. On November 20, 1972, Tommy went to Milledgeville State Mental Hospital, now known as Central State Hospital and he died on December 7, 1972, less than two weeks after his mother. Carolyn and Roy continued to live in the house until Roy died on June 11, 1975.

Echols "mini-reunion"
Eddie, Lester Smith Jr., Carolyn, me, Kappy, and Beckie Smith Johnson

At this time, Carolyn, who had been a very conservative woman, began to drink and hang out at bars with men. She sold the family home, quit her longtime insurance job, and moved to Chattanooga. One morning, I got a call from her; she had been committed to a hospital and needed my help. She wanted me to get her car out of the pound and help her get out of the hospital. I found out that she had cut her wrists and waited to die in her bed; blood was everywhere. I cleaned her apartment and then they released her. She wanted to stay in Chattanooga. I had mentioned earlier how she could really play the piano and violin; well, this was no more. I didn't feel comfortable about leaving her on her own. However, she insisted that she would be okay, and I had to take care of my responsibilities at home, so I left her.

It was only a few weeks later when another psychiatric hospital in Chattanooga called to tell me that Carolyn had tried to jump into the Tennessee River. This time, I brought her home with me to Atlanta. We were living in Dunwoody at the time. She stayed with us for several months and then got a job at a card shop downtown. She moved into a high-rise apartment, which certainly made me nervous. However, jumping out of the window was not her way to complete what she had tried twice before. On February 27, 1979, the Forsyth County Sheriff's Office called me because Carolyn had left my name and phone number on a note for them to call. I claimed the body. She had been found with a self-inflicted gunshot wound to her head and a bottle of gin next to her as she was lying on the bank of Lake Lanier. Carolyn lived such a tragic life.

In between Marie's death in 1972 and Carolyn's suicide in February 1979, I lost five other close relatives: Momma, Aunt Tankie, Grandmother, Daddy, and Aunt Buckie. It's hard for me to get all the deaths and hurtful days of the 1970s, but I will try. After Marie and Tommy died at the end of 1972, my daddy called me from Jackson, Mississippi, on January 18, 1973. He told me that Momma had had a heart attack in the middle of the night and was dead. Daddy asked me, "Can you come and help me?" I was stunned, but said, "I'll be there as soon as possible."

I was soon on my way to Jackson after I told Bob and the boys. When I arrived, I was really hurting; but when I saw my poor daddy, I totally lost it. What was he going to do? Momma had been taking care of him for almost forty-one years. Now he looked so old and weary. It didn't take us long before we were flying back to Atlanta with Momma in the cargo area.

Momma had had a heart attack about a year before this fatal one. Somehow, after we got back to Atlanta, we made the arrangements for the funeral. We even had to buy cemetery lots. Daddy and I decided to bury her in Peachtree Memorial Park in Pinckneyville, out close to Norcross. Some might not know where this "city" is. However, those who grew up in Norcross know that it is where the teenagers held drag races years ago on Medlock Bridge, out close to where Peachtree Industrial crosses it today.

After we buried Momma, my Aunt Tankie died of stomach cancer on February 19, 1973. Aunt Tankie had been an alcoholic for years. Then shortly after that, my grandmother Edith died on August 8, 1973, also of cancer. Grandmother liked to say she was "in her ninetieth year." She never drank alcohol, never smoked cigarettes, and worked hard on the farm. She lived by herself until the end of her life. Even though Grandmother was sharp as a tack until her death, Aunt John made her stop driving when she turned seventy! She outlived my Aunt John, who died of a stroke when she was only sixty on June 6, 1966.

Daddy came to live with us after we buried Momma. When I went over and cleaned their house, I discovered that Momma had been smoking in the bathroom; after her first heart attack, she told us she had quit. This made me very sad that those terrible things had such a hold on my momma and contributed greatly to her death. We moved Daddy's king-size bed and some of his things into our basement. He was lost without Momma.

Momma and Daddy's last picture together (1972)

Momma and Daddy had been friends with Earl and Molly King until Earl's death. Even after Earl's death, they still remained friends with Molly. She was one of the friends that Momma and Daddy were visiting when Momma died in Jackson. Molly had been a widow for a long time. Now that both were single, it did not take long for them to fall in love and marry. Although Momma had only been dead for about six months, I was glad they married because Daddy seemed happy again and had someone else to share his life. However, there was a part that really bothered me. Daddy treated Molly so much better than he had my mother. He opened doors for her, took her on trips, and just seemed to care more about her than he had my dear Momma.

This marriage only lasted eighteen months because Daddy had congestive heart failure in Jackson during a trip he and Molly took to welcome the New Year, 1975. After Daddy got released from the hospital, Molly asked me to meet the plane that brought Daddy back to Atlanta. I met him and took him to their apartment at 7100 Winter Trail, Apartment 15, in Doraville. Molly was going to drive back, so I was to take care of him until she returned.

There are two things that I regret during this time. First, I played tennis with one of my friends one afternoon at Daddy's apartment courts when I was there taking care of him. There was no problem, but I could have spent more time with Daddy. Of course, he insisted that I play. The other thing was stupid. Daddy and I were always open with each other, and he heard me on the phone. He asked me, "Who was that, and what's going on?" I regret my response even today, thirty-four years later. I said, "It's Eddie. He's in jail for growing marijuana in his yard." As if Daddy was not already in enough pain, this certainly didn't help his condition.

Daddy's main problem was blockage in the blood vessels in his legs. In fact, the arteries going to his lower extremities were nearly 100 percent blocked. They said his years of heavy smoking and high-fat meals, along with other factors, had caused cholesterol, scar tissue, and blood clots to build up inside his blood vessels. This problem of clogged artery disease, or arteriosclerosis, not only happened in his heart area, but Daddy also had had a hard time walking for years. The doctors called it peripheral arterial disease, or PAD. Since he was in so much pain, the doctors at Northside Hospital said his only chance of relief was to have surgery to unclog the arteries going to his legs. However, they said his heart would probably not be able to take it and his chance of recovery was very slim. Daddy had already had a massive heart attack in the spring of 1961, and unlike Momma, he did quit smoking. The doctors were right; he died on January 19, 1975, in the early morning. We had Daddy's funeral at Northwoods UMC and my good friend and our pastor, Reverend Don Harp, officiated. This still brings tears to my eyes today as I write about his death. Now here I was at thirty-six years old with both parents dead, one at sixty-two and the other at sixty-six.

The last loss our family suffered during these years was my Aunt Buckie; she lived until March 4, 1975. Buckie, also a smoker, had a drinking problem and ended up with diabetes and circulatory problems like Aunt John and Daddy. It was really strange because she had gone into the hospital with a toe she had stumped; it became gangrenous, so they had to cut it off. She died after the surgery from complications. She outlived my daddy by one and a half months.

If you've noticed, diabetes is very prevalent in our bloodline. My granddaddy Dan, Aunt John, Aunt Buckie, Daddy, and in my generation, Dodger and Eddie, had this horrible disease. Throughout my story, you will see me mention my love of sugar and my battle not to eat this killer. Well, in regard to my daddy's love of sugar, my good friend Carolyn often makes me laugh reminiscing how Daddy always had a big box of candy by his bed when she came over to spend the night during our high school days. We would lie up in his bed and eat candy with him. He always wanted to have this close to him! I can remember that even after he was diagnosed with diabetes, he would check his sugar level and then try to balance it with his insulin in order to have something sweet. Now my cousin Dodger does the same thing.

Yum-yum—sugar!

I went a year without sugar one time when we lived in Dunwoody. For many years, I have believed that it is a killer for me, and I'd be much healthier without it; also, my own diabetes could be just around the corner! Actually, my nephew Chuck has been off it for almost two years, and he has inspired me many times just to leave it alone. However, I keep falling off the wagon. I really believe that it is a drug, similar in nature to alcohol, which has certainly been a problem in our family as well. Quite possibly you have seen how so many relatives on both sides have had a problem with alcohol; that's one drug I have avoided. This might sound silly, but when Ken and Lane were in treatment, I went to lots of AA meetings, and when they talked about their relation to booze, I could relate my love of Coca-Cola. As a result of these meetings, I was able to stop drinking them in 1979 and have remained "clean and sober" all these years. I have told many people that I got off Coke in AA! Who knows—maybe I would have had diabetes by now if I hadn't.

Another weird thing about me was when I was about twelve, I stopped drinking coffee. Yes, Momma would give me coffee from the time I very young, but she put it in a glass of milk with lots of sugar. When I got older they stopped doing this, and I could never get it just right, so I started drinking my Cokes—morning, noon, night, and in between. Fortunately, when I got off my Cokes, I learned to like water, and for the last thirty years it has been my "drink of choice."

Reflecting on this period of my life, it is easy for me to see God's faithfulness during all these deaths. I know now that it's through difficulties that I draw closer to my Heavenly Father. I have written that I didn't get discipled after I accepted Christ as my Lord and Savior at twelve; however, I am grateful that I sensed that He was always there for me.

One great leap of faith came in March of 1973, when my pastor, Don Harp, taught a study on the Holy Spirit at Northwoods. The study was during Lent, and I remember actually giving up something in preparation for Easter. When I went to the altar at the end of the study, I asked God to take me and use me for His glory. This study became a real life changer for me. I finally realized He wanted me to surrender and allow the Holy Spirit to live through me. What I was giving up was—me.

Although there were no more deaths for a while after Aunt Buckie, it wasn't long until I realized there was something more painful than death—the drug days.

CHAPTER THIRTEEN

THE DRUG DAYS

No, I didn't do drugs; I went through this hell—sober. It lasted six years. After I prayed for God to take me and use me any way He wanted, this was just another step to know that I wasn't in control. This was the hardest lesson of my life.

Let's begin from the time Ken turned twelve or thirteen. Up until that time, Ken had been an ideal son. However, something started changing, and he was acting out, had a bad attitude, and his appearance was quite different as well. In the spring of 1974, he snuck off and smoked marijuana with his good friend Ken, who lived across the street. This was shortly before we moved to Dunwoody. My mother called him Kit Carson because he was always a problem in the neighborhood; you just didn't trust him or believe anything he said. Ken was a year older than Ken. Our Ken's personality really changed when he was fourteen. We just figured it was maturation and being a teenager.

We did not know about his using drugs until he was sixteen. By then, it was a full-blown addiction. He was out of control. We had moved to 1835 Vancroft Court in Dunwoody on August 29, 1974. It wasn't long after Daddy's death that I first caught Ken with marijuana. His bedroom was right across the hall from ours, and I saw him slide his hand up under his pillow when I walked into his room. I said, "Ken, what did you put under your pillow?" Belligerently, he said, "Nothing." Well, I didn't believe him and looked under the pillow—there was some Visine. I had read enough to know that this was used to clear the red out of your eyes after you smoked pot. He did admit it and said, "I just started and will never smoke a joint again."

This was in April 1975, right before his sixteenth birthday. I wanted to make sure, so I took him to our pediatrician, Dr. James; he told Ken how bad it was and really got his attention, or so we thought. We desperately tried to get help for Ken and our whole family; however, Ken was our main problem, and I was determined to fix him. We went to some of these therapists even before we knew drugs were a problem. In July 1974, we took Ken for a psychological exam, then to Dr. Ray Kukleburg for counseling. This was just the beginning; from 1974 until 1976, we cried out for help. We went to many places after starting with our pastor, Don Harp. Some of the places we went were the North Georgia Methodist Counseling Center (May-June 1975); the Link Counseling Center (May 1975-January 1976); Atlanta Counseling Center (August 1974-March 1975); and a nutritionist, Dr. William Saunders (July 1976). Unfortunately, none of these fixed Ken or me.

Like many other teenagers in our affluent community, Ken had his own car. My daddy had given Ken his old Pontiac Executive when Ken was only fifteen. Unfortunately, he had his first accident— following too close and ended up selling it and used some money that he had saved while working at Georgia Door and bought an orange 1969 Pontiac Firebird. By the time he was twenty, he had three DUIs—one on July 4, 1976; one on July 4, 1978; and one in December 1978. There was another arrest for public drunkenness in September 1978. In addition to these charges, in the summer of 1977, he had a charge for criminal damage to property in the second degree dismissed after he paid for the damages done to a car that he beat up because his friend had been fired from his job, and Ken felt the company had been unfair to him. This friend actually reported Ken to the authorities.

Through Ken's many offenses at Dunwoody High School, I met the assistant principal who was in charge of discipline, Robert Burns. He was always worrying about Ken's rebellious behavior. Ken's grades were terrible; he hung around with all the problem kids and caused many problems himself. He had no other choice but to go to summer school at Kittridge in DeKalb County. The school was many miles away from our house where all the druggies went. Ken decided to go there in order to graduate in the Fall. I was not going to take him. I got to the point of telling him, "I don't care if you ever graduate." And I meant it! Well, he showed me; He carpooled with three different friends Tim Hatshell, Jeff Cross, and Rusty Sayers and ended up passing. He was given a Dunwoody High School diploma in October of 1977.

Needless to say, Bob and I had been going through some very stressful days. He blamed me and I blamed him. One time, I went to my Aunt Kappy's house to stay. I just wanted to get away from all the heartache. Nevertheless, I did go back home after a couple of days. Here I was on a downward spiral, not able to control my firstborn son's behavior, and Bob and I were on the brink of divorce.

Meanwhile, our other son, Lane, had also started smoking pot with Ken. The first time was on the way to a swim meet in August 1976. Ken had told Lane that he would never push or pressure him into smoking pot with him. However, on this day Lane told him that he wanted to try it. When they got to the meet, Lane was too disoriented to race. By the way both sons were excellent swimmers and swam year round. They were ranked in Georgia for the breaststroke. Anyway, Lane was fourteen, and either we were savvier or Lane went downhill a lot faster. We later learned that Lane had crossed the line of addiction, lost control, and couldn't be careful as his big brother had been.

It didn't take long for problems to start. In May 1978, when he was fifteen and a sophomore at Dunwoody High School, Mr. Burns suspended Lane for smoking cigarettes in the bathroom. It's funny, Ken never got suspended for anything! Unfortunately to his own detriment or else he may have changed. Bob and I finally got our act together long enough to tell him that if he ever had another problem as a result of drugs, he would go immediately to a hospital, because we had been watching his brother go farther and farther down. We weren't going to wait for him to get better as we had hoped Ken would. Lane had been a good student, but by then, his grades were terrible.

Ken and Lane dressed up for my fortieth birthday—didn't
look like drug addicts/alcoholics!

Lane made it without another problem until December 8, 1978.
I will never forget that day. Mr. Burns called me that morning and
said,

"Lane is in my office and he won't let me see what is in
his hand. I need you to come."

I hurried up to his office, and before I got there, Lane had run
out of his office and stashed whatever he had been hiding. Mr. Burns
told me he was going to expel Lane but agreed to suspend him for
several weeks when I told him I was going directly to Peachford
Hospital in order to get Lane some help. That's exactly what we did.

We got in the car, did not go home, but drove directly to the hospital. He was only sixteen years old, and I committed him to the hospital to get help for his addiction. There was no adolescent unit then, so Lane had an old drunk for a roommate; nevertheless, Lane seemed to get along very well with this old man.

Believe it or not, I left Lane there and went to Peachtree World of Tennis to play my regular Friday afternoon match with my good friend and tennis partner, Jackie Huff. We played indoors every Friday with Jo Ann Nichols and Janet Turley. After we were finished, I told them about the day's events with Lane. They couldn't believe that Lane was in treatment or that I was able to play tennis without saying a word about the heartbreak of the day.

At eight o'clock that night, Bob and I went to our first Al-Anon meeting at Peachford Hospital. When we got there, I realize now, God had heard me crying in my closet for Him to help me; I didn't know what to do. As a mother who had loved and cared about her sons and would do anything for them, I learned in the first step that "I was powerless over alcohol, and my life was unmanageable."

There I was with my sixteen-year-old in rehabilitation. Finally, I had some people who understood what we had been going through. Even though I didn't know any of them, they loved me and really cared. As I studied the twelve steps in Al-Anon, I realized that it was a shortcut to the God of my understanding, the Triune God—Father, Son, and Holy Spirit. I already knew what the first step told me—"I was powerless"; the second step said that "God could restore us to sanity"; the third step said for me "to turn my life and will over to the care of God." Each step drew me closer to God. However, the eleventh step was a real source of help—"Sought through prayer and meditation to improve my conscious contact with God, praying only for knowledge of His will and the power to carry it out." How simple, but it was a wonderful revelation for me who had asked God to take me and use me for His glory not too long ago. Now He was giving me the tools to accomplish the desire of my heart.

That was our time at Peachford, and I say "our time" because they encouraged us to go to family meetings as well as Al-Anon. In fact, they told us we needed help more than Ken and Lane because we had been sober going through these stressful years. I understood I really needed help, so I went to ninety meetings in ninety days. This practice was encouraged in Al-Anon as well as Alcoholics Anonymous.

Not long after Lane was in Peachford, we had the opportunity to "persuade" Ken to join him. When he came before the judge, Ken was offered a choice of either paying a $1,000.00 fine and losing his license for five years, or completing a thirty-day treatment program. Ken didn't know we had gone to the judge and told him our son needed help. The judge also told Ken that he would write a letter to get his license back if he didn't have any more problems for one year. He agreed and went into treatment on January 2, 1979, after his New Year's celebration was over. On that day, we had both sons in a safe environment—not at home, but in drug rehabilitation. It was during this time that I found out that Ken had first smoked marijuana in March of 1974.

There were a lot of things I learned from my meetings and family therapies. One of my favorite counselors was Tom Haase. He told me in one of the family meetings that I had been playing God because I thought I knew what was best for everyone. Someway, I was able to accept what he said as truth. Years later, I read something that really expressed this truth in a vivid way: "What do God and controlling people have in common? They both love you and have a perfect plan for your life."

While the kids were in treatment, my life changed. I realized with the Al-Anon slogans—"Let go and let God," "Easy does it," "Take one day at a time"—and many other teachings that God was real, and even though I had been a Christian since I was twelve, my relationship with Him grew into a walk of knowing "I can't, but He can if I get out of His way and let Him." After I was broken, I told God to take me and do with me whatever He wanted; I had to die and surrender all to Him. For me, the twelve steps of Al-Anon showed me how. Thank You, Lord. I had direction, and I was willing. My faith was made stronger because He got me through those years.

Lane was dismissed on January 19, 1979. He had stayed in Peachford for six weeks and went back to school when he was discharged. Ken stayed the required six weeks and then asked if he could stay another week and a half because he had not really paid attention that first week. Of course, we said yes. Ken was dismissed on February 23, 1979.

By this time, I had begun to be very active in not only helping myself cope with two sons who were drug addicts and alcoholics, but I also began to reach out to other hurting parents. About this time, the Atlanta Narcotics Anonymous (NA) members were sponsoring the ninth World Convention of NA. They needed someone to start

Nar-Anon for the codependents that would be coming for this convention. Lois Wehunt and I rose to the occasion and started the first Nar-Anon Family Group east of the Mississippi River.

Early in our family's recovery, I went to a PTA meeting at our school where there were about 1,800 students. Mr. Stiegel, the principal, said that one-tenth of 1 percent had an addiction problem at his school. One father stood up and said he had one, and I stood up and said, "I have the other." I was furious; there were many hurting parents in that audience who didn't know what to do. Denial is a very significant obstacle in getting help.

Anyway, as a result of my openness, I met a very special person in my life, Tammy Sparks. She had two children and was having a problem with her son. She begged Mr. Burns to tell her if there was anyone else with whom she could talk. Well, he was reluctant because of confidentiality but finally gave Tammy my phone number. Tammy and I became best friends instantly. Tammy had met a young pastor, Ron Ross, who had come out of the drug world; and the three of us, on March 17, 1979, started a parents' group to help combat the drug problem in our community called Dunwoody Families in Action. Tammy and I went all over the state of Georgia sharing our stories and giving encouragement to parents, mostly at PTA meetings. We both got closer to God in our spiritual journeys as we watched Him work though us; we shared our lives in every opportunity He gave us. Sometimes we didn't even know what we had said when we were finished. It was absolutely amazing and a great faith builder.

Besides the Al-Anon and Nar-Anon programs, when Tammy and I were doing our talks, one of my main themes was that I had tried to be a good mom. Bob and I didn't drink, attended church regularly, kept the boys busy, and were there for our sons; nevertheless, they chose to use drugs. I told the parents, "It happened to me, and it could happen to you."

I was never ashamed of our problems and was very candid with anyone's questions. Many times, I shared some of my painful experiences. Here are a few: When we lived in Dunwoody, Bob nailed the windows shut in Ken's room because we never knew when he was coming or going.

One day we discovered that Ken had been hiding his drugs in his closet between the 2x4 studs covered by the baseboard. Ken said his brother got mad with him and hid the baseboard so we would see the hole in the wall. Then one day, before Lane started using drugs, I took him to a tennis tournament. When we got home one of Ken's friends, Jeff, was bleeding out on our front lawn. Ken later explained that he, Jeff, and another friend, Lindy, were gambling on a pool game in our basement and Jeff and Lindy got in an argument. They went upstairs to our great room when all of a sudden Lindy went into our kitchen, got a knife, and came after Jeff. He tried to get out of the house but Lindy caught him and pushed him right through our lovely front window. Glass went everywhere—including Jeff's back. An incident that after Lane started using drugs involved our Toyota. While Bob and I were out, Lane decided that he would take the car for a spin. Short story, he ran into a curb and the front axle was broken on one side. Lane got it close to home and asked Ken to help him push it into the garage. He then asked Ken "Do you think Mom and Dad will notice?" Ken said later he just laughed and said "Oh, yeah!" We did notice—right away.

The most lasting hurt occurred, in October 1976, when Bob, Lane, and I went to Knoxville, Tennessee to visit my longtime friend Jackie Villars Lane. We left Ken home with a house sitter; how stupid!

Ken had a party and one of his friends stole my grandfather Dan's gold pocket watch off the table in the great room. He also went into the bedroom and went into a drawer, then helped himself to the platinum diamond watch Grandmother Edith gave me for my eighteenth birthday. She had gotten it for her fiftieth wedding anniversary. The insurance company replaced it with a beautiful gold diamond watch, but it just wasn't the same.

Tammy and I had gotten involved with Sue Rusche, who was fighting the drug problem on the national level with Families in Action. She was going to be on a very popular television show called *The Phil Donahue Show*. Sue asked if Tammy and I would go with our families on the program. We considered it a great opportunity to share and were eager to go. Our whole family went, and the show was aired on March 9, 1979. This was a good time and a bad time. The topic was on kids and drugs. Ken was happy about his recovery; he shared how drugs had really messed up his life, and he was so glad to be clean and sober. This, of course, was the good; the bad was Lane. When he did not say one word, I learned later that it was because he was hungover. The night before, he had room service bring him booze and put it on Phil Donahue's tab. He thought he could sober up before the show; however, it snowed in Chicago during the night, and they woke us up early to make sure we got to the station on time.

We had already been suspicious about Lane's sobriety and decided that we would put him back into Peachford when we got home. On March 11, two days after the show, Lane was back in treatment. Even though this was his junior year in high school, his recovery was our main concern. Peachford thought that he was covered by insurance, and we had been paying our 10 percent. However, on May 26, 1979, they found out that he was not covered and felt he was well enough to leave. Peachford admitted their error and did not make us pay the other 90 percent! PTL.

After this stay, Lane was committed to sobriety, and shortly after his release, he was selected to go to the Governor's Honors Program in Macon on June 19, 1979. Lane had always been talented in art, and this was a great opportunity for him. Finally, something positive was happening in this young man's life. He maintained his sobriety through the six weeks that he was there in spite of the fact that the kids down there were doing drugs all around him.

Now back to Ken. Even though he had been so excited about his sobriety, when he got back with his old playmates, he fell back into his addiction. It wasn't long and he was facing his fourth DUI. However, he was charged with driving while being a habitual offender, which was a felony charge. We hired a lawyer, who arranged with the Judge to commute Ken's sentence if we got him some help.

I can still remember seeing Ken behind bars at the DeKalb county jail, then asking him if he was willing to go back to Peachford. He was very angry but agreed. According to the terms, Ken would be on probation for five years, and if he stayed out of trouble for those years, the felony would be dropped from his record. So on April 1, 1979, Ken is back in Peachford. But not for long—he admitted to the counselors that he had brought marijuana into the hospital and had been using and selling it to the other patients. The staff decided to expel Ken from treatment.

Ken came home and continued to have his ups and downs; we hoped and prayed that maybe he could make it. This was just wishful thinking. Even though he was still having significant problems, we sent him to North Georgia Tech to take drafting classes. This didn't last long. He started in October of 1979, and at the end of the first quarter, he had a B average. However, he was dismissed on November 20, 1979, for drinking alcohol in the student center one weekend.

We let him stay with us until after Thanksgiving; and then on December 3, 1979, Bob and I decided he had to leave. I was always playing the heavy, and I can clearly remember standing in the center of our kitchen, looking up into his eyes with so much pain in my heart. I said, "Ken, I love you terribly, but you have to leave our house. I can't help you, but God can, if I let Him."

It was nineteen degrees outside that night and he had no job, no home, and no transportation. We had taken his Pontiac Firebird to Fort Valley, Georgia, and asked my cousin Joan to keep it out on her farm. Ken had no idea where it was. We thought he left that night, but years later he told us that he snuck back into the garage and slept in the attic over the garage several days.

When I told Ken to leave, I told God that even if he got killed, I trusted Him to get me through it. I believed this was Ken's only chance to make it; nothing else had done any good, and we couldn't keep enabling him to continue doing his drugs.

In my mind, I knew this was the right thing, but my emotions were a basket case. The next day, I panicked and called Tom Haas, the counselor at Peachford. He reassured me that I had done the right thing and just to trust the Lord. I prayed and asked God to please let him move in with this wonderful Christian family that we had met at Peachford. Well, that is not where he went. Ken moved in with his drug dealer, Lawrence, and began selling drugs as well as using them. He was high all the time. This lasted until December 15, 1979. At that point, Ken was finally sick and tired of being sick and tired. A friend that Ken had met at Peachford, Tom Jones, approached Ken early on that December morning and told Ken he looked pretty rough. Well, I guess so—Ken told me later that he had been up all night drinking and taking crystal meth. Tom asked him if he would like to come live with him at his parents' home. Tom told him not to give him an answer then but to wait after lunch and let him know. At lunch, Ken told him he was ready to quit, and after work he went to his apartment and gave Lawrence the last of his crystal meth. Tom's family was the Christian family that I had prayed would take him in. Praise the Lord. Shortly after that, we told Ken, "When you have been clean and sober for three months, you can come back home."

Can you believe all the drama? Now we have to go back to Lane and his recovery. I mentioned that I had been doing a lot of programs around Georgia; Lane started going with me after he got sober. The last program that we did together was on October 6, 1979, for the Georgia Association of Educators, and he did really well. It was always special when he shared his story with adults and told them how prevalent the teenage drug problem really was. He also shared stories about his recovery. Shortly after this program, Lane had a problem with his allergies. He had always had a problem with allergies, particularly in the fall, so I took him to Dr. Moran, our pediatrician at the time. He prescribed Phenergan. I had asked the pharmacist if it were okay for an alcoholic and drug addict to take it; he said, "No problem."

This was wrong information. It contained alcohol, and on October 20, Lane relapsed. I called Peachford Hospital and asked them about the drug. They said, "Do not give it to him." I sobbed, saying, "Sorry, it's too late." Lane pretended to try to work the program, but it was evident that he was not. We told him that he would have to get sober again or get out. He left and moved in with one of his friends whose father was an alcoholic, and they all drank together. Needless to say, this didn't get the results we wanted.

Bob and I had heard about another program in Florida called Straight Inc. We decided to take Lane down there, hoping a different program could help him. On December 22, 1979, we drove to Saint Petersburg, Florida. It was a very strict program that required the teenagers to sign themselves in for a year. Lane was willing to be sober, but really was not comfortable with the approach they used and would not agree to sign the admittance form. I am so grateful that he didn't because since then there have been a lot of negative allegations about that program. Anyway, we brought him home, and he agreed that as soon as school started again after Christmas break in January, he would stay sober until he graduated from Dunwoody High School. We really believed that he could do it since he had been sober from March 11 until his relapse on October 20. We later learned that Lane's sobriety date did not begin right after Christmas break but on January 11, 1980.

Did you notice? Ken got sober before Lane! It was a most unusual New Year's Eve that year. Ken was so worried about Lane's being at a party that he wanted me to drive him over to the house where Lane was celebrating and he would go in and get him, which he did! Lane was very drunk, so we took him home. His sobriety was just around the corner.

CHAPTER FOURTEEN

LIFE AFTER DRUGS

Drug-free celebration on a Caribbean cruise (June 1980)

It is really amazing how my life changed after the drug days. The things that altered the most were my priorities. I was broken in my spirit, heart, and will. From that time on, I have recited Galatians 2:20 each morning. I no longer desired to do what I wanted, but wanted God's purpose and plan for my life. This change is hard to explain because, remember, I had always wanted to be close to Him and do His will. It's as if God put me through a training program to get to know Him better, personally. Of course, Al-Anon and Nar-Anon started to change my heart and truly seek God's will for my life. After that, I became aware of various Christian programs that allowed me to see my Heavenly Father clearly and learn more and more about His ways. One eye-opener was the "Walk Thru the Bible Seminar" on November 27, 1980. This is where I bought *The Daily Walk Bible* and began, at the ripe old age of forty-two, to read the Bible for the first time in my life! I couldn't believe it when I read through the Bible in only a year—it was so easy since it assigned which chapters to read each day. Then I attended the eighth Atlanta Christian Cursillo on November 21, 1981, after Bob had gone a couple of weeks earlier. Our whole family attended Bill Gothard's seminar, "Institute in Basic Youth Conflicts," on June 10, 1984. I had been attending many Bible studies as well; however, the ones that really helped me get into the Word were Kay Arthur's Precept upon Precept.

My heart also was changed toward the alcoholic. Before I experienced the drug days, I had hated alcoholics and wondered why they were doing this to themselves. The doctors at Peachford explained that alcoholism and other drug addictions were a disease, similar in nature to diabetes, and the addict did not want to be having these problems. Through this and so many other things that God showed me, I wanted to help the young addicts and their families. The next step I took was the most rewarding and fulfilling time of my life. I really felt I was in God's perfect will for my life. I could not believe the doors that He opened for me to walk through by faith. I started a teenage drug treatment program called the New Freedom Lodge (NFL).

Now you might wonder, *How in the world did she start a rehabilitation center?* Well, all I can say and know is that it was truly a God thing. I was willing to do whatever He wanted, and He provided everything for this to happen. I was able to attend seminars and learned so much that I got to be a certified addiction counselor. Then I spoke at seminars and conferences, in addition to the programs that Tammy and I continued to do. The head physician at Peachford Hospital, Dr. Conway Hunter, really took me under his wing. He knew the need for low-cost teenage treatment programs for so many families who couldn't afford private hospital care. Therefore, he really got behind me and encouraged me to start something affordable.

There was also a recovering alcoholic, Bill Walker, who was willing to help. Then there was this popular radio talk show host, Harry Davies, who had a problem with a daughter; we became good friends and he also encouraged me. Before I knew it, I not only had the heart, training, and desire, but also the confidence that God was enabling me to do this along with those He sent to help me.

A good friend and member of our tennis club, A. B. Martin, was a lawyer. He was willing to do all the legal work needed for us to be incorporated. So on March 27, 1980, New Freedom Lodge Inc. was born. AB established us as a 501(c) corporation, which enabled us to utilize tax-exempt donations. All that was needed now was a location. My vision was to use a church during the week when so many were empty. I needed to have a place donated in order to provide an inexpensive program for hurting parents to bring their teenagers. I continued to do my presentations with Tammy; we actually did over eight hundred programs at churches, garden clubs, schools, and civic organizations for anyone who would listen. At the time, I was a member of Northwoods United Methodist Church, so I went to my pastor. He took the request before our official board; I was stunned when the chairman, who had been a big contributor to the church, said, "No, this would not be a good idea because you would be using the stove and other things at the church."

I couldn't believe it! Next, I went to the district meeting and appealed to any Methodist church that would take us in— no response. I just kept trying, and then at the beginning of 1981, someone asked me, "Have you ever heard of a pastor named LaVerne Campbell?"

I said, "No, why?"

He said, "You ought to go see him. Maybe he can help you. His church is called Calvary Chapel Atlanta. It is located in an old school building in Sandy Springs."

I made an appointment with this LaVerne Campbell, and he seemed very excited about my vision. He actually said, "Well, I don't see why not. We have the room, and it sounds like something that is certainly needed in the community. I will bring it before my elders and see what they think. Then I'll be back in touch."

It was so simple when it was the right place. What a man. God really blessed me when he sent me to LaVerne Campbell. He was a man that really loved the Lord and people. LaVerne walked the talk. He also was like a coordinator in the Christian community; he knew everyone, and everyone knew him. Now to get our supplies in order, and I also needed a male counselor. Bill Walker had already told me he would volunteer his time because he had a real heart for the ministry of helping hurting families. He was on disability and would work for free. Bill had been in recovery himself for a long time and was really respected in the addiction community. Can you believe? So many times in my life, as I look back, God just takes care of me! Similar to what my earthly father had told me, "Charlotte, you can do anything you set your mind to and work hard." Daddy never really knew that whatever I could do was a gift from my heavenly Father. I also learned that He can get me through the good and the bad—just as Paul realized when he wrote:

"I can do all things through Christ who strengthens me"
(Philippians 4:13).

Thank You, Lord, for putting everything in place. The program was to be seven days a week for kids ages thirteen to eighteen. NFL was a program based on the twelve steps of Alcoholics Anonymous and on the teachings of Jesus Christ. We used both big books, AA's and the Bible. The patients would sleep at home but be at the center from 9:00 AM until 9:30 PM. We served meals at lunch and dinner. After preparing so many meals at church, cooking for the kids at NFL was no big deal.

On June 1, 1981, we were ready. Bill and I were waiting for our first patient. Another miracle—we got a call from a hurting divorced father whose fourteen-year-old daughter needed help. Before the day was out, we had our first patient, Tracy. She had done LSD at twelve and had a lot of issues. From then on, we helped many hurting families.

At one time, we had as many as twenty-three patients. I was still doing my programs and also served on the governor's advisory board for many years. One of the highlights was New Freedom Lodge's first anniversary dinner on July 9, 1982. Our guest speaker was Steve Bartkowski, the Christian quarterback for the Atlanta Falcons football team. We also had an up-and-coming Christian artist, Babbie Mason, sing. Another big occasion was when Nancy Reagan, President Ronald Reagan's wife, came to our center in March of 1982. She had taken a real interest in the problem of young people and drugs. Mrs. Reagan created the "Just Say No" campaign as part of the war against drugs. NFL was one of the treatment centers she visited around the United States. I also had the opportunity to visit the White House on two different occasions and became a member of the Nancy Reagan Speakers' Bureau. All of these extra activities I was fortunate enough to be a part of were never as satisfying as seeing a life changed when the young person became drug-free. Even today, I get so excited when I meet someone who has overcome addiction. I can almost see them as having come out of the grip that Satan had over them during their drug days.

Nancy Reagan, Pastor LaVerne Campbell, and me
at New Freedom Lodge (April 1982)

I had spent countless hours on the tennis court from the time Lane was a year old. I played at Oaks Country Club, as I have mentioned, with the guys, and then our club played other little neighborhood clubs. Some of these ladies told me about a league that was going to be played at DeKalb Tennis Center. This is where I met my friend Jackie Huff. She and I became best friends; we played the first year that the Atlanta Lawn Tennis Association (ALTA) had a league, in 1971. We really took tennis seriously, and as usual, I had to do my very best; that meant a lot of practice. After playing many tournaments and many seasons in ALTA, we played in USTA tournaments and even played a tournament in Charleston, South Carolina. In 1977, Jackie and I were ranked number two in the South because of how well we had done in this tournament and others.

Jackie Huff and me—notice the lovely bonnet!

However, one day after I opened NFL, a hurting mother called while I was out on the court. I decided that my competitive tennis days were over. I just had more important things to do with my life than play tennis. It's funny how God worked in my life because I never even considered that I was giving anything up! I was receiving by being able to help others. What a blessing and an opportunity.

Another blessing was when we needed to hire some more counselors; my son Ken worked for us part-time after he was living back home, clean and sober. He had met a young lady at Peachford named Rosita, with whom he fell in love. Things seemed to be getting back to normal.

During this time, I attended many conferences; one was the PRIDE conference at Georgia State University, April 8-9, 1982. At this conference, I met a young pastor named Steve Cason from Tifton, Georgia, and asked him to come sometime and talk to our kids. He said he would be happy to visit NFL. It wasn't long, and one day when Ken was working at the Lodge, Steve came and he was captivated with Steve. Ken said, "Mom, I have never heard anyone talk about Jesus Christ in such a way. I want Rosita and her friend Beth to go with me to visit him in Tifton."

So they went, and all three accepted Christ as their Lord and Savior on March 20, 1983. Rosita and her friend Beth moved to Tifton in the spring of 1983; Ken followed two months later. Steve ended up marrying Ken and Rosita on December 3, 1983, at Peachtree Road United Methodist Church. At the time, I had mixed emotions about Rosita; Steve had asked whether we approved of Ken's marrying her. Then I still believed that Ken should marry her because they had been having intimate relations for quite some time. Remember my thoughts about how God saw this? Therefore, Bob and I said yes, knowing that she was not the most responsible person and was immature. It sounds funny now, but I really felt sorry for her and also realized that Ken was not the most mature, responsible young person either. This combination was to come back to haunt us in a few years.

We had our last board of directors meeting on February 28, 1984. The Lodge closed shortly after that, or I should say God closed the doors to NFL, just as He had opened them that first day. Every now and then I ask Him why.

One thing which should not have interfered with NFL was our move to Cumming on September 25, 1983. The real reason NFL closed, I believe, was my Aunt Kappy. You remember she was my momma's older sister. She had stepsons, but never had any children of her own, and I had always told her that I would take care of her if she ever needed me. At this time she really needed me because she had esophageal cancer. Kappy had also been an alcoholic, but had quit drinking after Momma died in 1973; she knew Momma had always worried about her and was led to stop when Momma died. Here it was ten years later and Kappy was very sick. They did chemotherapy, and I can remember feeding Kappy through a tube going down her throat into her stomach. Kappy had always been such an independent person, so this time in her life was very difficult. She sold her house and moved in with us so I could take care of her.

Our Cumming property had been a special blessing from God. When we bought seventeen acres on Highway 141, one mile south of Highway 400, for $225,000, it seemed like a lot of money; and to us it was, considering we did not sell our Dunwoody house at the time. Bob really wanted it, and I liked it as well. It was a 2,400 square foot house. There were two bedrooms on the main floor with a full basement that looked like a bowling alley. The exterior and much of the interior was cedar. This was a very dark house, but I did remodel it, trying to make it more appealing and brighter.

Bob always thought I wanted to leave Dunwoody, but really, I loved my life in the house that I built. There had been some complications with our neighbors because we had Alcoholics Anonymous meetings on Sunday afternoons in our basement, and they didn't like "those kinds" of teenagers coming into our lovely neighborhood! Of course, Ken and Lane had been here all through the drug days, but now the neighbors thought they were a problem. One day, my next-door neighbor asked me to come to a meeting at her house; there were about ten other neighbors there. They were really upset and wanted the AA meetings to stop. I told them I would pray about it and let them know. This was one of the few times that I asked God to show me in His Word what we should do. I opened the Bible to Romans 16:17-18, which told me, "Now I urge you, brethren, keep your eye on those who cause dissensions and hindrances contrary to the teaching which you learned, and turn away from them. For such men are slaves, not of our Lord Christ but of their own appetites."

So I wrote them a letter the next day which told them that we would continue to have the meetings. This did not make our neighbors happy, but Bob and I were in agreement on what to do. I really believe Bob is a lot more sensitive to matters like this, and he was hurt. For some reason, I can accept rejection and know I am okay! This was in the spring of 1980, and from that time on, we looked for someplace to settle down; as it turned out, this was in Cumming, Georgia. We believed that we would build our warehouse for Georgia Door in the front yard; the house was in the very back of the seventeen acres. However, it was determined that the grading would cost more than if we bought property elsewhere more suitable and built. We bought a little more than two acres at 955 McFarland

400 Boulevard in Alpharetta, only one exit from our house. We moved the business from downtown Norcross to this new building in January of 1985.

Early in the 1980s, we started attending Calvary Chapel North. The pastor was David Grubbs, who had been an elder with LaVerne at Calvary Chapel Atlanta, where New Freedom Lodge had been. Soon, we were really involved with Calvary Chapel North. They had been looking for land after meeting in a school for several years. Bob and I felt God wanted us to give them four acres of our property. Shortly we had our church in the front yard after the men built a debt-free church building. This was great; we had lots of meetings in our home, and I could even walk to church. I especially loved having the buffets at our house after the Christmas Eve candlelight services. This tradition has continued to this day. All of our friends know we have an open house the Friday before Christmas, and they bring a favorite dish. I was preparing everything until one year I ran out of food, which was understandable since I didn't know who or how many were coming!

I really believe that God provided the space and environment for Kappy to spend her last days with us. She loved her flowers as I did, and I was grateful that she got to see her transplanted Lenten rose bloom just before she died. During the time Kappy was living in our house, I connected with my mother's family. We attended the Echols' reunions together at Haw Creek Baptist Church in Cumming. These were fun, and I actually found where my great-great-grandfather, W. N. Blackstock, had been the pastor at this little church in the mid-1800s. Reverend Blackstock was the father of my maternal great-grandmother, Hannah Jane Blackstock, who married James Ewell Echols.

Earlier, I had told the tragic story of my Aunt Marie, the oldest daughter of my grandparents, Perry and Carrie Echols. However, the second child, Pearl, was a completely different story. She married Lester Smith from Dalton, Georgia, and had my cousin Rebecca "Beckie" Smith Johnson from Rome, Georgia, and her brother, Dr. Lester Smith Jr., a dentist in Cartersville, Georgia. Beckie and Lester Jr. had grown up in a close Christian family. My cousin Lester Jr. was born on June 7, 1933, and died on April 17, 1995. His older sister, Beckie, was born on December 27, 1930; she and I are now closer than any of my other relatives. She is such an encouragement in my life. We still try to have our little Echols family reunion every summer at my house. It is strange how I really feel connected to Momma's side because Beckie and her children—Jennifer Ostenson and Bob Jr.— and Lester's children—Carrie Brown from Birmingham, Alabama, and Lehman Smith, from Cartersville, Georgia—have such strong walks with the Lord. It was exciting to get to know family members who know Christ. I had never experienced this before, although I always felt and knew that my grandmother Carrie was a strong believer, and I really believed she had prayed her children and grandchildren would come to Christ, including me.

Echols family reunion 1997

I am in the center; daughter-in-law Karon, holding Juliana, to my right; Jacqueline in front between Karon and me; cousin Beckie is to my left. Lane directly behind me and Bob on far right. Ken in second row, left end, with Jessica next to him and Kelley in front of them

Unfortunately, Momma's one brother, Alton P. Echols, was an alcoholic who went into the navy at an early age. We lost track of him and his family. He married a lady named Aileen and had a daughter named Barbara. My Aunt Kathryn never mentioned having a relationship with the Lord and never went to church.

All of these new connections and life in Cumming certainly changed my life. Throughout my life, it seems there were periods of peace; and then all of a sudden, things were not the same. This was again a time for new interests and finding what God wanted me to do next.

CHAPTER FIFTEEN

GOD, TELL ME WHAT TO DO NOW

Okay, NFL was closed; Kappy was in the extra bedroom at the Cumming house. We had the spare bedroom because Ken was in Tifton and Lane had chosen to leave our home the year before when we were still in Dunwoody. Oh yes, he was clean and sober but kept coming home late, and finally, I asked Bob to talk with him. After Bob talked with him, I asked, "Well, what happened?" Bob answered, "I told him if he was not in the house by 4:00 am, he couldn't drive the car for two weeks." I didn't say anything; for one thing, I was too stunned, and also, God had been teaching me about the husband being the head of the home. Anyway, Lane couldn't abide by this curfew, so he had to leave our home! Can you believe? This was September 1982; Lane had maintained his sobriety for almost two years, but he had a bad attitude and was rebellious.

In 1983, even though Lane was not living at home, he was still working at Georgia Door. About a year after he moved out, he and Bob got into a big fight at work. His girlfriend, Heather, knew he was really confused about his life and was searching to know what he believed about God. Shortly after this, Heather broke up with him; that was another blow for Lane. He was at a very low period in his life when Ken called him out of the blue at 2:00 AM and told Lane that God told him to call. Lane had lots of questions. He did not believe in God, but he later told me that he cried out to God to reveal Himself, if He really existed. Lane decided to go to visit his brother in Tifton. This was in the fall of 1983, and on October 23, Lane accepted Jesus Christ as Lord and Savior. His was a dramatic conversion; he was a new creature in Christ, just like the Bible talks about in 2 Corinthians 5:17: "Therefore, if anyone is in Christ, he is a new creation; the old has gone, the new has come!"

Wow! What a blessing. Praise the Lord. He came home to live. He even gave all of his secular music to his friend Andy. From that time on, he didn't need a curfew. Lane attended Bible studies and church at Mount Paran Church and read his Bible in the unfinished basement area we fixed up for him. Remember, Aunt Kappy was in the spare bedroom. He was always home after his meetings, and his whole countenance changed.

Not only did Lane start doing better at home; he also did better in school. God put it in his heart to go to Auburn University (the new name for my old Alabama Polytechnic Institute!) for a degree in engineering. Lane had been attending DeKalb Junior College and Georgia State University as an art major and was on scholastic probation when he got saved. He now wanted to transfer to Auburn and the School of Engineering. Lane had always been great in math, except for during the drug days. What would it hurt to try? Lane and I drove over to Auburn on May 30, 1984, to talk with the dean of the engineering department. Lane had sent his application and his transcript with a GPA just under 2.5. The dean looked the transcript over and noticed that in the fall of 1983 and spring quarter of 1984, he had made the dean's list with a 4.0 both quarters after being on scholastic probation. He asked Lane what happened, and Lane said, "I got saved, and it changed my life." The dean then said, "Lane, we normally require our transfer students to have a 2.5 GPA, but even though you are a little under it, I am going to give you a chance to show us what you can do. I am accepting you to Auburn for this summer quarter. And I want you to take chemistry, physics, and calculus."

Lane went to Auburn, and that quarter he got two As and a B. He decided to "co-op" and live at home every other quarter while working for IBM. Lane went on to graduate as an electrical engineer in 1988. On May 11, 1998, Lane got his MBA from Emory University. Thank You, Lord.

Someone else I need to mention was our good friend Brother Russell Aaron Clayton. He's part of Lane's story, so I'll introduce him here. Within six months after Lane's conversion, he attended a leadership conference that Kay Arthur had at her ministry's facility called Reach Out Ranch, in Chattanooga, Tennessee. This seminar strengthened his walk with Christ. It is also where he met Brother Russell, who our family grew to love through the years. Brother Russell was a very meek human being. In fact, when Lane met him, he was in the cafeteria eating alone; Lane felt sorry for him and started talking with him. Lane became friends with Brother Russell and invited him to stay with us when he came to Atlanta. Brother Russell was an amazing gentleman with an unbelievable testimony. He was a Spirit-filled Jew who was converted to Christianity when he was fifty years old. His whole life was extraordinary and is probably much too long to explain in my autobiography, but I will try briefly.

Bob's Aunt Joy Sampson Hatfield, Brother
Russell, me, and Bob (December 1986)

Basically, Russell was the son of a Jewish mother, from the tribe of Levi, and an English father. He was born in England on July 14, 1914. Russell was educated in Europe as well as the United States. He spoke seven languages and had a PhD in history. Brother Russell was an accomplished pianist who even played in Carnegie Hall. While he was living in Germany in the late 1930s, he played for Adolf Hitler. Brother Russell had gone to rabbinical school and knew the Old Testament thoroughly. However, with all this worldly talent, once he accepted Christ, he only listened to God and obediently followed His orders for his life. From that point on, all of his talents were used for God. When we met him, his only possessions were his books that people had given to show their gratitude for his visit; everyone knew how much he loved his books. He traveled the roads with truckers from city to city and coast to coast sharing the gospel with whomever God showed him. One time, we asked him why he never married and he explained that he was born a eunuch and never had sexual desires for a man or a woman. When Russell was saved in 1964, he was drunk and thought he was in Chicago. However, he had gotten on the wrong train and ended up in Atlanta. An angel of God spoke to him in an audible voice and that night his life was changed.

Lane was in school at Auburn when Brother Russell called us for the first time. He needed a place to stay and asked if we could pick him up way down on the south side of Atlanta. This would be the first of many visits through the years. That's what he did; we never knew more than a day ahead if he was coming to visit us. Just think, he didn't know where he would be laying his head to rest from day to day. I can hear him now, saying, "Sister Charlotte, can you meet me at the library in Canton tomorrow?"

We would pick him up and let him stay at our house as long as he wanted. Lane had told us about this amazing man, and we were blessed by his presence. All his free time was spent reading the Bible and seeking a closer and closer relationship with his Lord. Many times, I would invite friends over to share Russell's insights into the scriptures with them. He truly blessed others and me with so many of his teachings and wisdom. He was so intelligent that it was inconceivable to him that I could not understand something that was so obvious to him! We'd be sitting at the kitchen table, and I would ask him a question. He would say, "Now, Sister, you know that."

Something else he made me appreciate were God's daily gifts to each one of His children. I can remember his saying, while looking at a beautiful sunset glimmering through the trees, "Sister Charlotte, look at that beautiful sunset. Did you know God made that just for you and me because we're the only ones enjoying it?"

Brother Russell died on February 13, 2009, at the ripe old age of ninety-four. He died in the home of one of his supporters; we were so grateful he was not out on the street somewhere. I attended his funeral three days later at the Owen Funeral Home in Cartersville. Many of his friends from far and near attended the service. It was a happy celebration for a life lived for Christ; several stories were shared that we could all relate to. Some told about how Russell loved ice cream and would make special requests but humbly tell us that he didn't want to be a burden. All of us agreed that he was an amazing child of God. He truly blessed me and my family through the years.

I continued seeking to know God's will, taking one day at a time. Regardless of any period in my life, I always have a full platter before me. I like to think that it's what God wants me to do, but sometimes I'm not so sure. After the Lodge closed and Lane was at Auburn, you would have thought I'd have plenty of spare time; however, this was not the case. I remained very active in the drug rehabilitation scene. The county commissioners asked me to serve as chairman of the Forsyth County Substance Abuse Commission. I was still serving on the governor's advisory council and doing many talks for different organizations, along with taking care of my Aunt Kappy.

God also was revealing Himself more and more to me through His Word. After Bob and I attended the Atlanta Christian Cursillo in 1981, we got very active in a similar weekend event called Tres Dias; there are two in the Atlanta area, and we have served in both the North Georgia and Georgia Mountains Tres Dias events. We have really been blessed with these three-day weekends and have also served in Walk to Emmaus, a similar three-day weekend sponsored by the Methodist Church, as well.

Since I was chairman of the Substance Abuse Commission, I got to know Sheriff Wesley Walraven and, later, Sheriff Joe Robertson really well. They both allowed me to go into the Forsyth County jail. They had very few female prisoners, but my friends—Carole Pittman and Bert Cain—and I would go there every week and share Christ with the ladies. During this time, there was a very special lady, Twilya, who I got to know and love. She had a serious drug problem, as did most of the ladies in jail, and when she got out she accepted Christ and was baptized in our little swim spa on our porch. Our swim spa had been used by Calvary Chapel North for all the baptisms.

Churches offer hope of change to inmates

FORSYTH COUNTY
NEWS — Sunday, December 5, 1993

JAIL from 1A

By Lee Johnson
Staff Writer

Members of local churches have joined efforts in a mission to one of the world's more isolated locations, the county jail.

"When people are in here, their families don't have a lot to do with them," said Joe Robertson, a lieutenant at the Forsyth County Detention Center. "The people who come to minister to them have almost become surrogate families for them. They offer one-on-one counseling, study the scriptures, talk about problems. They're a shoulder to lean on, and someone the inmates can relate to. It takes a special person to do it. These people are very dedicated, and that's what it takes."

In the past, several of the churches have offered programs to the inmates, but last summer, church members saw a need for a more coordinated effort. They formed a committee to to help meet inmate needs more efficiently.

"The programs are still offered by the individual churches," said Charlotte Czekala, member of Calvary Baptist North, "but now we share information so we can communicate to others (churches) what we're doing,

and we can see what services are available in other churches. We all share the common goal of getting the Word to the inmates and letting them know that people care."

Services offered by the individual churches and coordinated through the committee include the donation of clothing and Bibles, Bible study, counseling, and non-denominational religious services held at the jail.

Recently, the committee also enlisted the help of Greg Cox, a professional substance abuse counselor currently working with Forsyth County Mental Health. According to Czekala, Cox will begin a substance abuse program at the jail this week.

Czekala said administrators at the detention center have been "just wonderful", supporting their efforts, allowing them to bring in materials, informing them of jail procedures, and even acquiring new meeting room space.

"We made some modifications to the old uniform assembly room in the fire department building," said Robertson. "We added a few walls to make a multi-purpose room. Now we can comfortably seat around 27 inmates."

According to Robertson,

See JAIL, 2A

inmates previously met in a visitation area that could accommodate no more than four people at a time.

Czekala stated that before the jail added the new meeting room, church members were "actually ministering through the bars."

The ministering church members visit inmates on a regular basis, some several times each month, some every week, according to Robertson, and inmate response to the programs has been positive and is growing. He believes that part of the reason for this success is that the ministers give the inmates hope that they can turn their lives around.

"Two of the people that come in are former inmates," said Robertson. "These guys can accomplish more in one sermon than a trained professional can in six months. The inmates see someone who has been here before, and has risen above it and changed their life, and it gives them hope."

> The people who come to minister to them have almost become surrogate families for them. They offer one-on-one counseling, study the scriptures, talk about problems. They're a shoulder to lean on, and someone the inmates can relate to. It takes a special person to do it. These people are very dedicated, and that's what it takes.
>
> —Lt. Joe Robertson

My "mug" picture to get to go to jail
and article in the *Forsyth County Newspaper* regarding
our ministry to inmates (December 5, 1993)

Twilya agreed to go to a Tres Dias weekend. However, when Bob and I went to get her, she was leaving with a guy. My heart was broken and aching for my dear friend, who was drawn back into her old lifestyle of drugs and sex. I kept track of her for several years by calling her Aunt Doris, but the last time I saw her, it was rather awkward. I went into the restaurant where she was working and she was pretty withdrawn. In my mind—Satan won.

Of course, Aunt Kappy took up a lot of my time, but God provided a young woman, Nanette Klinect, to help me. I met Nanette at NFL when she was a teenager. She was a member of LaVerne's church and came to visit our girl patients. When we moved to Cumming, she and her husband, Paul, were living across the street from us. They were expecting their first child. Nanette helped me many days with Aunt Kappy. One of those "God coincidences" was her baby Peter being born on the day Kappy died, March 14, 1984. That morning, I wondered why Kappy was not up. When I went into her room, she was dead on the edge of her bed.

After Kappy died, my life continued with the same activities that I had been doing before her death. However, something else that I had always wanted to do was travel. Since I had such great memories of traveling with my daddy, I always had a desire to see the world. This opportunity came later that year, and we were able to go—thanks to a small inheritance from Aunt Kappy. Mount Paran Church's choir was invited to sing at Manger Square in Israel on Christmas Eve 1984. Wow, what a trip! Bob, Ken, Rosita, Lane, and I got to go with them. None of us could sing, but they invited anyone who wanted to come along for the trip. Another couple that we really loved, Frankie and Bobby Patterson, were also going and it just happened their daughter, Karon, was also coming. Frankie and I thought Lane and Karon would make a perfect couple.

I tease now that Frankie and I had already picked out our mother of the bride and mother of the groom dresses when we introduced them at New York's LaGuardia Airport. However, they didn't take to one another too quickly. In fact, Lane was wearing a wool sport coat and was sniffling as a result of his allergy to wool. Not a good first impression. At a certain point, Karon mentioned that she was going to call her boyfriend, Michael, and tell him goodbye before our plane departed for Israel.

In spite of all this drama, we had a great time seeing the Holy Land, where Jesus was born, lived, died, and rose again. After we left Israel, we got to tour Europe for a week. We landed in Vienna, Austria, on New Year's Eve on the way back to the United States. The small van that we had rented was waiting for us at the airport. It was very cold, but we piled into the van with our luggage and took off to see the world—well, as much as we could see in seven days.

It was even very cold in our van, but we headed out for Italy. However, it was late that night; and we took a wrong turn, ending up in communist Czechoslovakia. The guard at the gate was drunk and was waving us into his country—no way! We took a quick U-turn and finally got to our hotel in Italy for the first night. That night was the first time I had seen a bidet, which I thought looked weird. Besides Italy, we also went to Germany and Switzerland. Not bad for a week. It had to be fast because I didn't know if I would ever get to come to Europe again.

After we returned home, Lane went back to Auburn, and Ken and Rosita went back to Tifton, but not for long. Shortly after our trip, we realized that the ministry Ken and Rosita were involved with in Tifton had some serious problems. What seemed like a really wonderful Christ-centered ministry got sidetracked, and Steve was enforcing questionable rules, especially on the women; he would not allow them come home to visit or communicate with the outside world. So in 1985, Ken and Rosita came back to Atlanta and moved into our basement apartment for a while. Ken started working for Georgia Door.

That summer, Ken and Rosita invited Lane to go with them to White Water Park, an amusement park in Marietta. Lane asked me, "If I invite *that girl* to go with me and ask her to pay her own way, would she think I was asking her for a date?" I said, "I don't think so. Why don't you go on and ask her?" Well, he did, and as they say, the rest is history. They were together all the time, and on June 7, 1986, Karon and Lane married at Mount Paran Church. Frankie and I got to wear our dresses! Lane had not yet graduated from Auburn, so he and Karon lived in the condo we had bought for Lane while he was attending Auburn.

Lane and Karon's wedding
Rosita was pregnant with Kelley, Ken was best
man, and Bob and I were proud parents.

Rosita was a bridesmaid at the wedding, although she was pregnant with Kelley Grace. My first granddaughter was born on November 22, 1986. Just three weeks before this event, Ken and Rosita had bought a house at 1530 Crestwood Court in Alpharetta. Then only eighteen months later, on May 29, 1988, our second granddaughter, Jessica Anne, was almost born in Ken's car but made it to the emergency room at North Fulton Hospital. Wow! I was truly blessed with two precious granddaughters. Life was good.

Life got even better. Karon and Lane blessed us with another granddaughter, Jacqueline Leigh, on June 11, 1991. Jacqueline is athletic and excelled in swimming, both in the summer leagues and during high school at King's Ridge Christian School. She was the captain of the team and had a great breaststroke and freestyle. I can still see her dive starting a race; it was the best. She would dive almost over halfway across the pool before she would surface to take a breath! Jacqueline won many ribbons and trophies and was one of Georgia's best for many years. She also likes to have fun, enjoyed dancing ballet until her knees hurt, and was a lifeguard during high school. She plans to attend Covenant College, like her mother.

Then along came Juliana Lane on June 8, 1995. Julie, as she likes to be called, is fun-loving, loves animals, has an easygoing temperament, but her passion is horses! At this time, she has six of them in our pasture. She outgrew one of them—her feet were almost dragging the ground, but she hated to part with Duncan. Juliana is already our tallest granddaughter and is still growing. I won't be surprised if she gets to six feet like Frankie, her maternal grandmother. She looks quite beautiful in those horse shows, sitting so straight with her lovely slim body.

I kept saying I deserved all these girls after raising those two boys. Now another surprise—a grandson! He was born on March 23, 2001, named John Coleman, after Karon's maternal grandfather and, of course, my wonderful father. What a blessing. In so many ways, Coleman reminds me of Daddy with his laugh, great smile, love of life, love of sports, love of card games, and math brain (also like his father and me!). He seems to have a great awareness of how God wants us to live, and I pray he will live a life for God. While we are talking about children and grandchildren—I kept hoping that one of my offspring would have my blue eyes, but nada (just to show you that after all my hard work, I do remember some of that difficult Spanish!).

Here is a picture of the grandchildren and our precious dog, Buddy.

Buddy, Juliana, Jessica, Coleman, Kelley, Jacqueline

During these years, I resumed my regular routine: church, jail, Georgia Door, yard work, tennis, and even cooking. One thing Bob and I decided to do was buy a condo on the Gulf Coast. So on Labor Day in 1988, we bought two condos at an auction—units 1205 and 1206 at Beachcrest in Santa Rosa Beach, Florida. Wow, did we get a bargain—both for $150,000!

There was no drama during these years. However, in 1991, Rosita started looking for her biological parents and found them. This was the beginning of trouble. She first found her mother, Judy Ferraro, and then her father, Milledge; neither had ever married. Rosita's biological parents had been teenagers in high school when Rosita was born, and Judy went to the Florence Crittenton Home for unwed mothers; there she gave Rosita up for adoption. Celestina "Chelo" Merino from Cuba and Dr. Ignacio Merino from Spain adopted Rosita.

CHAPTER SIXTEEN

COMPLICATIONS

From the time Rosita found her biological father, things changed, and the complications began. While Judy had been a blessing for Rosita, her father was a problem. This, of course, is my own view of how their little family fell apart; however, whoever remembers these times will wish they were different. Rosita had already started some negative behavior. She and Milledge had a lot in common. It was an exciting relationship, and Rosita was soon committed more to her father than Ken and their family. Temporary separation came on October 21, 1992. Ken had not been the perfect husband and father but was willing to try. Jessica was four and Kelley was five years old. I had asked Ken if he was sure that divorce was necessary, and he felt it was. I talked to Rosita, and afterward, I had to agree; she wanted out.

From that point on, Bob and I were fully committed to helping Ken get custody of the girls no matter how much it cost, and it did cost a lot—about $35,000. In the end, we did win custody. However, this was not a satisfying win because the girls lost a chance of a normal family that would love and care for them. During the hearings, the court asked Bob and me if we would be willing to help Ken with the girls, and of course, we said we would. From that time on, my life took a detour.

I have often had desires or goals in my life, and one came to mind after the final divorce in February 1994. I had always wanted to have two boys and two girls, with the boys being born first. Well, here I was a "mother" of two girls born twenty-four years after the two boys. I'm sure Kelley, Jessica, and Rosita would resent my term *mother* in my relationship with the girls; but I really felt more like the mother than a grandmother. In fact, I felt shortchanged because I was not able to experience the fun side of my relationship with them as a grandmother. Someone, had to get them up, teach them, discipline them, take care of them when they were sick, take them to the doctors, get them braces, get them eye glasses, take them wherever they needed to go, clothe them, and the list goes on and on. I was Grancie, and Bob was Grang Grang; they knew they could count on us.

Meanwhile, Ken was busy with work and dating; Rosita was in her new world with her father. However, I have to give Rosita credit; she did visit with the girls when it was her time and in her own way loved them. Her visits drove me crazy because I was at her mercy, and she was always late, especially when she was picking up or dropping off the girls for her visitations. According to the divorce agreement, she should return them to Ken's house and not mine; so many nights, I had to sit out in my car at Ken's house when he was out of town to take them back to my house. There seemed to be many very cold and rainy nights! I was often jealous because she was more like the grandmother and just having fun with them.

In 1994, the pastor of Calvary Chapel North (CCN), David Grubbs, wanted to buy our house and the other 10.23 acres. We agreed to the selling price of $450,000. Bob and I took a note for $317,000, the balance after the down payment. Our new house was to be in Cherokee County, close to our friends Kellum and Cara Tadsen.

By the way, we served as counselors for the Billy Graham Crusade at the Georgia Dome October 26-30, 1994. He was a great evangelist, and we were fortunate to hear him preach in person. It was a real blessing to serve this magnificent man of God.

Part of the agreement with Calvary Chapel allowed us to live for free in the house until I finished building our new house. We bought fourteen acres in Cherokee County, which was out in the boonies but sounded closer in part because it had an Alpharetta address. We paid $18,000 an acre. There was a pasture in the front and a lake in the back. We moved in on April 13, 1996, and the next morning, God gave me an unexpected blessing—as I opened my eyes and looked out, the sun was coming up over the lake. Then later that day, the sun was setting over the pasture. The views were absolutely beautiful—morning and night. It had taken me fifteen months to build the house even though it wasn't that big. I also built a swimming pool that was twenty feet by forty feet, just like my Aunt John's; it even had a diving board. By then, we had been taking care of Kelley and Jessica for almost four years. Each of the girls decorated her upstairs bedroom. It was truly my dream home, with a large deck overlooking the lake.

My dream home at 1516 Gantt Road, Alpharetta, Georgia

I say it took me fifteen months to build the house, but I want you to know that building the house was very similar to starting and running a drug treatment center. About the same time I started building the house, I went into a Catholic bookstore and saw this little plaque that said, according to Hebrews 3:4, "For every house is built and furnished by someone, but the Builder of all things and the Furnisher is God." I bought it and have kept it in the kitchen to again remind me of His faithfulness in taking care of me. One example of His faithfulness while building the house was in the very beginning, when about twenty Mexicans came to pour the foundation. I saw them running around everywhere looking for the sand! Well, this great builder had forgotten to order the sand, so lo and behold, they all left. I was so sad but finally got another worker to lay the foundation; he told me if we had poured the footings where they had been dug, the house would have been laid out incorrectly. Thank You, Lord. Together, we built a dream house and it has blessed us so much. We had a big party and dedicated our home and all we had to the Lord. As a result, we became the swim and tennis club for the community.

Bob's mom, Florence O'Brian, was planning a visit not long after we moved into our new house; however, she was not physically able. She died on July 11, 1997. Although Flo was not a big part of our lives, whenever we went to Chicago or she would come to Atlanta, she was always a very pleasant and loving mother, grandmother, and mother-in-law.

As another side note, 1996 was a very busy year for me! I had both of my knees replaced in February, finished building the house and moved in in April, took a vacation to Hawaii in May, and attended many of the Olympic events that were held in Atlanta in July.

In 1997, CCN started having problems. We started going to Little River Church that met one mile from our new house. One of the elders from CCN, Dan Becker, started it in the old one-room schoolhouse that had become the Union Hill Community Center. Not long after this, in 1998, CCN church defaulted on the note; and we got the house back and 10.23 acres. Since we were already living in Cherokee County, we tried to sell the property and finally did in September 2005. We sold the ten acres for $120,000 an acre, PTL. It was the first time in my life I had ever felt rich. Although I was born during the Great Depression, I don't remember our family needing anything. Not that we had abundance, but always enough. However, a truth that I was taught and tried to practice throughout my life was

"Waste not, want not." Now that I was really rich, maybe I could waste! (Just kidding—being frugal was too deep in my bones.)

Since Kelley and Jessica had been so involved in our lives, I want to share some of the thoughts I remember about them during that time. When Kelley and Jessica were very young, they seemed to really depend on each other and were very close. Probably after the divorce, this was even more the case. Bob and I sent them to Redeemer Christian School; then Karon and I homeschooled Jessica during the fourth to the sixth grades. Ken gave Kelley the option of going to public school for sixth grade and she went to Hickory Flat Elementary after we had homeschooled her for one year. After that, they attended Horizon Christian Academy. Kelley and Jessica were athletic and played basketball. Both girls were very competitive and even though Jessica was very short, she went after whoever had the ball and didn't worry about how big they were. It was fun to watch her attack!

Both girls were quite beautiful. However, their physical development was on both ends of the spectrum. Kelley was fully developed at eleven and Jessica started maturing at sixteen. I mentioned that Jessica was very short playing basketball, but by the time she was seventeen, she towered over her sister. A funny story about Jessica was how we would take the grandchildren to the go-carts at the beach and there was a little sign that read, "If you are this tall, you can drive the go-cart." Well, I believe Jessica got her Georgia learner's permit before she could drive the go-carts! Kelley and Jessica had great personalities and never met a stranger.

While they were in high school, they both lifeguarded at Wills Park in Alpharetta.

Kelley studied piano for several years and continues playing. This blesses me, especially because you remember my momma played the piano all through my growing up years and she could play anything you could hum. I think I already told you I was tone-deaf and had no rhythm, but fortunately, Kelley didn't take after me in this area. Even to this day, I love to hear piano music. Jessica also studied the piano but really liked dance, and that is what she has continued to enjoy even after she was on her own. She has always been very graceful and quite flexible. Kelley ended up graduating from Horizon Christian Academy in Cumming, and Jessica chose to go to Sequoyah High School for her senior year and has graduated.

A couple of years after we moved into our new house in 1996, we gave Ken and Lane four acres on each side of us and kept six acres in the middle. Ken sold his home on Crestwood Court in Alpharetta and moved into our garage apartment until his house was completed in September 2000. He also had his office for Summit Building Products in his basement. Kelley and Jessica moved out of our house into his. Yes, life was different. He lived there until October 2009 when he moved to Fort Myers, Florida. He had lost everything—business, house, cars, etc. The United States had a really terrible economic recession, especially after the election of Barack Obama.

After Kelley graduated from Horizon Christian Academy in May 2004, she went to Southeastern University in Lakeland, Florida. Bob and I drove her down there. Encouraging Kelley to go off to college was a big mistake. The school was wonderful, but Kelley was just not ready to be on her own. She always had a hard time in school, and this new freedom allowed her to become involved in activities that were detrimental to her life. Kelley stayed there one year before coming home and then she worked as a nanny for two years. She lived next door to us with her father and Cassiana, Ken's wife from Brazil. They married on August 16, 2003.

Ken and Cassiana's wedding
L-R: Lane, Jacqueline, Kelley, Juliana, Cassiana,
Ken, Jessica, me, Bob, Karon, and Coleman

Living with Cassie and Ken didn't work out and Kelley moved back in with us, trying to get direction for her life. Kelley worked many odd jobs and eventually moved out on her own.

Jessica took a few years off after graduating and started to attend college last year at Perimeter College in Dunwoody while she worked at a dance fashion store for two years. Bob and I bought a condo for Kelley and Jessica in December 2007. The condo was in Jessica's name because she was the one with credit and qualified for the loan. Kelley never understood this, and with other things going on in her life, she chose to leave the condo. She lived in various places until she came back to live with us again this past year. That didn't last long; she wanted her independence.

You might notice I have not written that "life is good" for some time. It seems after the divorce and my involvement with Kelley and Jessica, life stopped having that carefree element that I had felt when I was younger. It was most difficult trying to take care of the girls while both the mother and the father were not so happy with the arrangement. My life was not my own, and I was not able to control many aspects of it. Something I had learned in Al-Anon kept running through my mind. It is called the Serenity Prayer: "God, grant me the serenity to accept the things I cannot change, courage to change the things I can, and the wisdom to know the difference."

This was and is still not easy for me to put into practice. In my mind, I know that I cannot make people do what I just know would be better for their lives, but I keep trying. There is another saying that I learned in Al-Anon—"Insanity is when you keep doing the same thing over and over expecting different results."

In the therapy groups at Peachford many years ago, I remember Tom told me that when I believe that I know what's best for another person's life, I was playing God. Now I believe God's message for me is to trust Him and get out of His way. I used to sing a song to Kelley and Jessica every night after we would say their prayers. Kelley's was "Kelley Grace, Kelley Grace, puts a smile on my face, how I love my Kelley Grace. She is my first granddaughter, and I love her so. I thank You, Lord, for Kelley Grace. Kelley Grace, Kelley Grace, be obedient, be obedient to the Lord God, for He's got a plan and a purpose for your life and He knows what's best for you." Jessica's was "Jessie Lou, Jessie Lou, how I love you. Jessie Lou, Jessie Lou, I love you. You're my second granddaughter, and I love you so. I thank the Lord for Jessie Lou. Jessie Lou, Jessie Lou, be obedient, be obedient to the Lord God, for He's got a plan and a purpose for your life and He knows what's best for you."

Then we would end with one verse of "Jesus Loves You." Often, I think about this ritual that we had for many years and think, *Don't they know He's got a plan and purpose for their lives and His ways are best?* Then I think, *Charlotte, do you really believe this as well? If so, trust Him. He's got the plan and purpose for their lives. Let Him have them! Remember, they are twenty-three and twenty-one years old now.*

Yesterday, I wrote how God was dealing with me, and today (August 25) the meditation in *Jesus Calling* was:

> I am the Eternal I Am; I always have been, and I always will be. In My Presence you experience Love and Light, Peace and Joy. I am intimately involved in all your moments, and I am training you to be aware of Me at all times. Your assignment is to collaborate with Me in this training process.

I have taken up residence within you; I am central in your innermost being. Your mind goes off in tangents from its holy Center, time after time. Do not be alarmed by your inability to remain focused on Me. Simply bring your thoughts gently back to Me each time they wander. The quickest way to redirect your mind to me is to whisper My Name.

How long will it take? I know that trials and tribulations draw me closer to Him—my helper and comforter. I know in my mind that I need Him every moment. However, most of the times, I forget to call on Him for help. Therefore, my greatest plea is "Lord, help me remember You—who supplies all my needs."

During the separation and while their family was being torn apart, I was blessed by knowing that both Kelley and Jessica trusted Jesus Christ as their Savior. Kelley on September 9, 1991, and Jessica on November 16, 1991. They both were baptized in my swim spa at the Cumming house by their father and Dan Becker on Kelley's birthday, November 22, 1991. Jessica was baptized again in the Jordan River when I took Kelley and Jessica on a trip to Israel in January 2008.

CHAPTER SEVENTEEN

HEY, REMEMBER MY LIFELONG GOAL?

During the years that I took care of Kelley and Jessica, from 1992 until I taught Kelley to drive when she was sixteen, I really didn't think too much about what I wanted to do. I really enjoyed many of the activities that we shared in their school and also the extracurricular activities, as well as just having time to be with two precious girls, but after Kelley started driving in 2002 and living at home with Ken, my job was over.

Another job that was over was Bob's. He retired on December 31, 2000. I gave Georgia Door to our nephew Chuck. This wasn't an easy decision, with Ken and Lane both wanting the company. However, Chuck had been a loyal employee since he was fourteen years old and was certainly very capable of running the company. Now looking back on it, it was the right thing to do. He has done a great job and has paid Bob's retirement every year. He has also given me a bonus for many years as well. I believe my daddy would be very proud of his grandson, who overcame growing up with my sick brother as a father. Chuck is the third generation to benefit from Daddy's company. Hopefully, his son Jayson will be the fourth, if Georgia Door can survive this terrible recession in the building industry. President Obama's change is not working. He made so many promises, but in my opinion, he has gotten our country in a big mess. The housing industry, which Georgia Door is dependent on, took a nosedive. The foreclosures and quick sales are everywhere. I think anyone would be foolish to build a new house when so many people have lost theirs to the bank and you can buy very nice houses—cheap. Ken's house was a good example. When the bank took over his house, it had about a $1.2 million value and was sold in foreclosure by the bank for less than $500,000. Also, the debt that was incurred during Obama's administration was a big problem and many are concerned that our nation could end up bankrupt.

Of course, with his retirement, Bob was home full-time! Woe is me. I can remember one day, not too long after he retired, he asked me, "Charlotte, did you water the plants today?" I thought to myself, *Yes, and I've been doing it for over forty years, thank you very much.* Little things like this helped me decide what I wanted the next phase of my life to be!

Along with my wanting to get married at nineteen, I also always wanted to graduate from college. Well, I was not a brain and didn't know what I was thinking! Remember, I went to LSU in 1956 and Auburn in 1957. Well, guess what happened in 2002!

The first thing I did in January was start drinking Pat's [Robertson] Age-Defying Shake. This was delicious, and for the first year, I drank it every day. I would blend nutritious things like soy protein, whey protein, strawberries, ice cubes, "mother's vinegar," lecithin, MSM, and flax oil that Pat had in his recipe. Well, I lost forty pounds that year and twenty the next. By the way, I had a tummy tuck on

December 9, 2004, to shed all three pounds of loose skin, along with my appendectomy and hysterectomy scars. Get this, *Dr. Pound* told me I was the oldest person he had operated on for a tummy tuck! I don't believe I told you that I was 5'8¼" when I got married and weighed 156 pounds. Through the years, when I couldn't exercise because my knee problems got so bad, I weighed 220 pounds; on top of this, I started shrinking and was only 5'6" when I last measured! After my knee replacements in 1996 and the fact that Kelley and Jessica were not relying on me, I started taking care of Charlotte and lost the sixty pounds with this drink and exercise. My biggest deal was returning to college, where I also got a personal trainer—free!

It was remarkable how it happened. There was a garage sale in our neighborhood on Gantt Road, and I stopped to see what they had. I love garage sales and anywhere else I might find a bargain. Anyway, at this garage sale, I got to talking with a neighbor lady that I had never met before. She told me she went to Kennesaw State University. By the way, I never have trouble talking with people, and did we talk. I told her about my lifelong desire to graduate from college; she told me to get registered, and we could ride together to KSU. I really thought this was a possibility and decided that I would try to get more information. I called Kennesaw, and they wanted all my transcripts, even my Sacred Heart transcript. Yes, I got them and even found my high school transcript at the Atlanta Catholic Diocese. This was not easy since Sacred Heart closed in 1958.

So here I was, so excited; and would you believe, I called this new friend, and she had not been able to get the classes she wanted and wasn't going that semester! By then, I was already registered and had my classes scheduled, so I was going on my own! On August 27, 2002, which just happened to be my sixty-fourth birthday, I went back to college. I was so fortunate because they transferred all of my credits from LSU and Alabama Polytechnic Institute (later Auburn University). I was especially grateful for the B in the calculus class that I had taken so many years before when I was a physical education major with a math minor at Auburn.

I felt very emotional on that first day back. There were many thoughts going through my mind. First, I was very grateful and full of excitement, then not believing that I was really there, and, finally, wondering if I could really do this. Would my brain work again? Oh yes, I had been watching the History Channel on TV and taking notes because I was so interested in history. And yes, I had homeschooled and helped the girls with their lessons, but this was different—I had to take the test and write the papers. Oh, brain—oh, brain, where art thou? I knew one thing—I would do my best, and if the Lord wanted me to be a college graduate, I could and would do it.

A college student on my sixty-fourth birthday!

The first test I can remember getting back was in Dr. Elango's world history class. When he returned the papers, tears started running from my eyes. One of my young friends asked me what I got, and I told him, "I got an A." He was surprised and relieved, and I was so grateful, realizing that I could do it! This was something God did for me over the next seven years. He gave me the desire, the brain, the discipline, the financial means, and all the support of friends and family through those years.

When I started again, I knew I really loved history, and therefore, I majored in world history and never thought about changing my major again. Another gift God put in my path was a lady who became my dear friend, Gayle Wheeler. Gayle was the assistant to the chairman of the history department, Dr. Howard Shealy. Gayle was also a nontraditional history student who helped and encouraged me throughout my seven years at KSU. She graduated in 2006 and I went to her celebration that night. She had written on her cake that she had gone on the forty-one-year plan. I figured at the time that I would graduate on the fifty-four-year plan because I believed that I would finish in 2010. Fortunately, it only took fifty-three years, thanks to the five wonderful summers I spent, studying abroad!

A highlight of my time at KSU was being an ambassador. I was very fortunate to have met a lady named Dotty during my first year at school. She was an ambassador and encouraged me to qualify. I was accepted in 2003 and served KSU at many events and functions. It was fun; and I got to know our presidents, Betty Siegle and then Dr. Papp, as well as many students through the years. This was my way of enjoying campus life and joining in.

Some of the things that stand out in my mind about the last seven years at school are the many trips that I took. Bob and I had the opportunity of going on some wonderful trips with Grand Circle Travel. I convinced Bob that since I was a world history major, I just had to see the world. During this time, remember, we had all that money to do whatever—and the "whatever" for me was to travel. Bob and I went to Turkey, Australia, Fiji, New Zealand, Egypt, Greece, China, Cuba, and Brazil.

Bob and me in Turkey (May 2003)

I also persuaded Bob to let me travel on study abroad programs with KSU while he stayed home and took care of our yard and wonderful dog, Buddy. The first one was in 2005; I studied in Madrid and lived at the Colegio Mayor Universitario de San Pablo. It was a very affluent boys' boarding school, and we lived in their dorm during their summer break; it even had a pool and tennis court. I loved Madrid. The weather was wonderful, clear blue skies and no humidity! It only rained about one hour during the five weeks I was there. I had my own private room in the dorm, but I noticed that when I was going to bed at night, the other students were just leaving for their night out on the town. Nothing started happening in Madrid until after dinner at about 10:00 PM. However, I did get my Spanish credits and had my first geography class with Dr. Harry "Dr. T" Trendell. I would have three more classes with him and he was one of my favorite professors. The teachers encouraged us to travel on our long weekends, and I did go to Marrakech, Morocco, and Lisbon, Portugal, on two of my weekends. All through my college days, the other kids really accepted me, and I loved many of them. Madrid let me have my best friends of them all. They were really good young Christian girls, and we even had a great Bible study with about one-fourth of the students attending, even many guys. I have many fond memories of that trip. One highlight was when they took me to the Hard Rock Cafe. It was wild. Life was good. I haven't said that for a while!

In 2006, I went to Oaxaca, Mexico, and lived with *mi madre*, Gloria, who only spoke Spanish. I wasn't sure what my accommodations would be like; I even packed toilet paper in my suitcase! What a pleasant surprise—her house was beautiful, and I had all of the conveniences of home. Gloria was a widow who was about ten years younger than I, but on the first day of school, I had my backpack on my back and she was walking me to school; as we approached the road in front of the language school, she took my hand and walked me across the street. The whole five weeks were like that. No, she didn't walk me to school each day, but she did cook and care for me as if I were her child. And yes, at the language school, they only spoke Spanish. For four hours, five days a week, I was in the classroom. Nevertheless, I did finish my Spanish requirements in order to get my degree in world history. I took this Spanish course early in my studies because I wasn't sure if I could pass the five semesters that the history degree required. I really felt if I studied hard I could pass the other subjects, but it had been almost fifty years since I had studied Spanish! These proved to be my hardest classes. However, I made two As and three Bs in Spanish. The only way I could make even Bs was by studying really hard on what I could do—vocabulary, writing, reading, and conjugating. I was awful at speaking and understanding when they talked to me. But I did it! Oh, I forgot to mention a wonderful tutor, Natalia Martinez, from Colombia. I met her in the language lab at KSU and then she became my personal tutor. We are still good friends and often go to the movies and out to eat. I love Natalia; we also have tennis in common. She is working on becoming a citizen of the United States. Well, anyway, finally I really began to believe that I would be able to graduate from college.

The next year, 2007, I went to Saint Petersburg, Russia. Again, I lived in a college dorm called IMOP. This was another wonderful experience. I shared a suite with another student, Tracey, but I had my own bedroom. IMOP had Ping-Pong tables on the first floor, so I got to play quite a bit. I was always good and the young people were fascinated that this old lady could beat so many of the kids!

I met and established a lasting friendship with our director's wife, Mindy Webb, from Bainbridge, Georgia. She had a son, Brady, in the program. I loved the whole family, and although they were Mormons, I felt a kindred spirit with them in their relationship with the Lord.

In the summer of 2008, I went to Montepulciano, Italy, with Dr. Howard Shealy. I'm not sure if it was my favorite program because each program had its special attributes; however, it was wonderful. I had the opportunity to live with a professor from Georgia Southern University, Dr. Patricia Price. We had this beautiful old two-bedroom apartment that overlooked the Tuscan landscape. Can you believe? Montepulciano is located on top of a mountain and the views were spectacular. I also remember getting a lot of exercise while hiking up and down this mountain to school and back. The apartment had a small kitchen, and I was able to cook some for myself. However, we had our dinners five nights a week at the wonderful small Italian restaurant very close to our apartment. The restaurant was Trattoria di Cagnano. The word *cagnano*, "the big dog," is the name of the neighborhood where the restaurant was located. Dr. T and his wife, Kay, were also on this trip; and I got to take another geography class with him. He really believed you could learn more from the top of everything; so he enjoyed taking me again and again to the highest points in every city, including the domes of cathedrals in Rome, Florence, and any other place under the Tuscan sun!

This was the first time that I was asked to socialize with the professors, which was special. However, I really enjoyed eating with four of the young people that sat at my table each night—Clint,

Margaret, Lindsey, and John. At the other tables, they kept ordering wine, while at our table, we ordered bottled water. We would save the caps and build a pyramid, trying to beat our record of twelve bottles! We were all Christians and asked the blessing before our meals—what an odd group, but we had fun. Of course, one of the highlights was going on field trips two days a week. We went several times to Rome and Florence, but also Siena, Pisa, and Assisi. Oh yes! I did get to play a lot of Ping-Pong in the center of town under the big tent. I beat guys from our group, Italians, even Dr. T and many guys from Albania who had migrated to Italy for jobs. Ironically, a sixteen-year-old Italian boy clobbered me. Some of the kids had arranged for him to play me; he was really good. Oh, I must mention the gelatos; I just loved that Italian ice cream! I could never find one in the USA that was as good.

My last study abroad was during spring break this year, 2009. I went with about twelve other students to Belize, in Central America, for an anthropology class. This trip was my least favorite excursion. The professor, Dr. Terry Powis, was not very well organized and did not take very good care of us. I believe that the worst thing he did was to encourage me to go into the Actun Tunichil Muknal, or commonly called the ATM cave. Now remember I was and still am a very adventuresome seventy-year-old lady with both knees and both hips replaced. However, there are some things that would be stupid for me to do—for instance, jumping out of an airplane, going snow-skiing, or in this case, going into the two-thousand-year-old Mayan ATM cave in Belize. Dr. Powis knew of my handicaps, but did not forewarn me about this cave and actually encouraged me to go! It was a guided tour and our tour leader was a Belizean named Jamaal. It was supposed to be an hour-and-a-half trip into this cave; well, it took us almost three because of me. There were places in there where I had to climb cliffs and go through rough terrain covered with freezing water. I was happy about some of the places with freezing water because I could get off my legs and swim! If it hadn't been for Jamaal, I don't know if I would have made it. After I had climbed some of those cliffs that were sometimes twenty feet high, I would have to trust him to catch me as I literally leaped into his arms. After it was over, I can say I really enjoyed the view inside the cave, but it was stupid for me to have done that!

Before I went on this trip, I petitioned to graduate and had been approved to graduate in July—that is, if I passed my spring and summer classes. Life is good, and I did complete all of my requirements, which leads me to the next chapter . . .

CHAPTER EIGHTEEN

OH, HAPPY DAY, FINALLY

There I was, seventy years old and so excited. You see, on July 30, 2009, I graduated from Kennesaw State University with a bachelor of arts degree in world history. When I started writing my autobiography for my nonfictional writing class this past spring semester, I had decided to have my graduation as the grand finale for my story. As you can see, it has taken me many more pages than the fifteen to twenty that my professor wanted me to have for that class. So I asked a very special professor, Dr. Elsa Nystrom, if I could finish my story with a directed study for the summer semester of 2009. She agreed and gave me my syllabus. Lo and behold, she had listed eight books for me to read and then meet with her to discuss the questions she had assigned regarding each book. All this work before I could finish my autobiography. Oh, I couldn't believe it; I was such a crybaby. I said, "Oh, Dr. Nystrom, eight books? You know what a slow reader I am, and I so wanted to complete my autobiography." She had no mercy and said, "Oh, Charlotte, I have to read the same books you do, and I know you will enjoy them. You will be able to complete your autobiography after you read the books. And you'll be better equipped."

Well, she was right in one regard; I did enjoy most of the books, which were all autobiographies. Included in her list were autobiographies by Kirk Cameron, Maya Angelou, Babe Didrikson Zaharias, Arthur Ashe, Barbara Bush, Loretta Lynn, Amy Tan, and the only one I really didn't like, Eudora Welty. Although I didn't get through with all my story, she told me that eighty-four pages was enough, along with how well I had done on my reading assignment, and that I would receive an A for the class. Hopefully, she was also correct in believing I would be better equipped to write my autobiography! So I didn't get started on this chapter until after graduation and then went back to fill in the chapters from "God, Tell Me What to Do Now."

Now I am finally a college graduate. It only took fifty-three years from the time I started in the fall of 1956 at LSU. At last, I accomplished this lifelong goal. I have shared with you my adventures as a nontraditional college student, and I am so grateful to God for giving me the desire, ability, and resources to complete this dream.

I must tell you that I was awarded many honors for my studies. When I returned to school after almost fifty years, I wondered if my brain would be able to rise to the task. All I can say is that I did my very best. In fact, on every test, I reminded God that I had done my best and the rest was up to Him. That might sound a little disrespectful on my part, but I did depend on Him to get me through the hard times. I graduated magna cum laude with a 3.86 GPA. The only Bs I had were three in those doggone Spanish classes and one in a lower-level elective that I chose to take in the spring semester 2009—Psychology 1101! It was interesting, and I loved my professor, even if I ended up with an 87 in his class. Of all the honors I received, the one I am most proud of is for Outstanding Student for the Global Initiatives Department. I received it because of my GPA and the fact that I had gone on five study abroad trips.

At graduation, I had all of these ribbons, cords, and medals around my neck, and on top of my cap, I put PTL. My family and many friends attended and cheered very loudly as I walked across the stage to receive my diploma and a hug from our president, Dr. Papp. I was so excited, but I only cried before the ceremony when we were walking across the street from the old gym into the Convocation Center as a lady played the bagpipes. It was wonderful.

Two of my friends, Tracy and Gloria Hattaway, came all the way from Fort Walton Beach, Florida. My two best friends from high school, Carolyn Schaeffer Galvin and Gail Rogers Crawford, also came. We took our fifteen-passenger van so Sam and Rosemary Badgett and David and Priscilla Craik from our small group at church could ride with us along with Kelley. My cousin Dodger, Ken, Cassiana, Jessica, Paul, Nanette, Olya, and Aaron Klinect met us there. What a group, but it was small in comparison to that night's celebration. Lane, Karon, Jacqueline, Juliana, and Coleman had been vacationing in Maine the week before and had to come home early to join the festivities. Their plane was delayed, but they got to KSU just in time for pictures!

I had reserved the Union Hill Community Center, where Bob and I had celebrated our fiftieth anniversary in July 2008. Cara and Kellum Tadsen and their girls—Brekken, Hope, and Joy—had been preparing for this event, along with my cousin Beckie's daughter, Jennifer Ostenson, and, of course, Karon, who spent many hours fixing the flowers and table decorations, washing tablecloths, and cleaning up the mess. In addition, Juliana, Jacqueline, and one of their friends, Alex Clanton, blew up two hundred helium balloons. I almost forgot—our guest of honor (besides me) that Karon got. It was this neat life-size figure of Elvis Presley. As you can see, this was quite a big event, and many of my family and friends spent hours preparing a very special time for me. Over one hundred came to celebrate this grand occasion with me that night. Joshua Whitmire played music from the golden oldies. Everyone seemed to have a great time, and I was truly blessed. Can you believe—a college graduate at last! Life was good again.

Family outside Union Hill Community Center
L-R Juliana, Jacqueline, Karon, Coleman, Kelley,
Bob, me, Lane, Jessica, Cassiana, and Ken

Another surprise happened after my graduation—well, not exactly a surprise since I called our local paper, the *Cherokee Tribune*, and asked them if they were interested in my graduating at seventy years old. They called back and did a great article about my graduating. However, the next thing that happened was a big surprise: Channel 5 News called and wanted to interview me for a news segment for television! So on August 31, 2009, I was on their news program; and later, I found out they ran the segment for several more days. They set up the interview by our lake after my seventy-first birthday.

Grandma graduate

Charlotte Czekala, 71, of Union Hill fulfilled a lifelong dream this summer by earning a bachelor's degree in world history from Kennesaw State University. She graduated magna cum laude and won the Outstanding Student Award. According to the school's dean of enrollment, the number of students age 60 or older who attended classes over the past few years ranged from 58 to 72.

■
Photo special to the Cherokee Tribune

Article published in the *Cherokee Tribune*
on August 28, 2009, right after my seventy-first birthday

Many people have asked, "What are you going to do now?" or "What are you going to do when you grow up?" They even asked me this during the interview. All I know to say is that God has a plan and a purpose for my life and that I'm willing to do what He wants. I really don't know, but I am looking forward to no more book reports or exams. I would like to become a better reader; those who read seem to understand so much more what's going on in the world. One thing I know is that teaching really excites me, especially teaching tennis, swimming, and bowling.

We joined North Point Community Church on June 13, 1999. This is an exciting church to be a part of, even if the music is "wild." Our pastor, Andy Stanley, is a great communicator and founded the church to attract those who are lost and don't feel comfortable in church. As a result, we have many who come and sign up for the Starting Point ministry where I have been a leader for six years. SP is where returners, seekers, and starters come one day a week for ten weeks to have a Bible study. We encourage them to share their life with us and for them to feel comfortable in asking anything. This is encouraged by the leaders' transparency. It is wonderful to serve here. Our church's mission is "to lead people into a growing relationship with Jesus Christ." Starting Point certainly does that by providing "a conversational environment where people can explore faith and experience community." Hopefully, I will continue to be involved with God's work for me at North Point.

Another thing I want to do is attend more Al-Anon meetings. I got such help and continue to get help by helping others who are hurting from the same pain that I went through so many years ago. Looking back on my life, I know that raising a family was very important to me; however, the most fulfilling time was when I founded and ran New Freedom Lodge. I really felt closest to God and His perfect will for my life during those years. This is something I will not be able to begin again. It took a lot of energy and direct enablement from God to do that. So at this point, I will catch up on many things at home that I have been putting off for the last seven years and hopefully wait on the Lord for His perfect will.

EPILOGUE

Someone else will have to write the end of this story. Here I am, seventy-one years old, and only God knows how many more years He will give me. Something that is really on my mind is our great country, which was founded by Christians. America has been a blessed nation. However, with this last election in 2008, Obama ran on change, and change is happening. I didn't want his kind of change. Time will tell whether it's for good or for bad. For your sakes, I pray for good.

Up until now, you have read how many blessings and challenges I have lived through. I believe that most would agree that overall I have had a very blessed life. Even though the trials have been painful, once I was through them, they served as faith builders. My goal is to realize this contentment in all things *during* the trials. This is just a matter of trust, and I start every day praying, "I believe that You can meet my needs, and I trust You, Jesus, to provide this day. Protect me. I want to live a day of trust in You."

As I consider these times, God has never left me nor forsaken me. As Job 13:15 wrote, "Though You slay me, I will trust in You." I have written this book for my children, my children's children, and all that follow. It is my prayer that I will see you in heaven. I have prayed for your salvation; you are redeemed through Jesus' blood. Accept His sacrifice and let Him live through you. I pray that each of you will have a close walk with God our Father. Remember, just as I sang to Kelley and Jessica, "He has a plan and a purpose for your life, and He knows what's best for you. Jesus loves you, this I know, for the Bible tells me so."

May God bless you and keep you, my precious ones.